STEVE WALSH

Growing Older with God

RISE OF THE SAINTS EMERITUS

Copyright © 2019 Steve Walsh

All rights reserved. No part of this publication may be reproduced, distributed, or transmitted in any form or by any means, including photocopying, recording, or other electronic or mechanical methods, without the prior written permission of the publisher, except in the case of brief quotations embodied in critical reviews and certain other noncommercial uses permitted by copyright law.

Published by
EVANGELIONS LLC
17503 La Cantera Parkway
Suite 104 - 174
San Antonio, Texas 78257

www.evangelions.org

ISBN: 978-1-7334336-0-0 (EBook)
ISBN: 978-1-7334336-1-7 (Softcover)

Scripture quotations taken from The World English Bible ~ Public domain.

First printed edition 2019

Henry J. Walsh
1924 - 2014

Marilyn J. Walsh
1928 - 2019

Contents

Introduction

America's senior citizens are suffering. Some struggle silently in moods of mental depression, while others groan quietly in bouts of physical pain. They are slaves to medical practitioners, consumers of fistfuls of medications and hopelessly dependent upon expensive healthcare insurance. They are disturbed by their declining ability to control things in the world around them. They hunger for help beyond another medical diagnosis or a government promise. They see their hopes and life passing them by. They yearn for answers to cope with what their life has become. The poor among them feel fear, and the rich feel nervous. The elite feel untouchable.

You hope that you are different. You pray that old age will pass you by. At the very least you think old age will treat you differently. Maybe some force of nature will allow you to snow ski at the age of eighty, or sky dive at ninety. But in reality you know that something is changing. More and more you are losing your balance. Occasionally you trip over an imaginary ripple in the floor. Sometimes picking up an item takes an effort you don't remember ever needing.

At first you hide the subtle changes from your family. You laugh it off when you get confused about something. You tell people to speak up. You make jokes about aging. You tell everyone you will live to be a hundred. But deep down inside you fear that you are just a few steps away from a walker with tennis ball glides. Gradually, ever so reluctantly, you come to accept that you are being consumed by the inevitable. For the first time in your life you fear you will become another face in the invisible millions forgotten by the world, perhaps by your own family.

No matter who we are, rich or poor, great or small, man or woman, gay or straight, smart or dull, devout or atheist, some of us will grow older. It is God's great equalizer that puts people at humble parity with those who have gone before them into the shadow of the valley of aches, pains, and eerie uncertainty.

Yet we are not frightened of death. Given the alternatives we would welcome a quick death. It is the prospect of years of suffering that nibbles away at our soul. It is the idea of being humiliated, or mocked that creates an unwanted anxiety. Our thoughts of lingering pain betray a deep-seated fear of our mortality. For the first time in our life we think seriously before answering the doctor when she asks if cancer runs in our family.

Then, one day a close friend says that they are downsizing. They tell us that they are moving into a retirement home. They say it will be good. But we know different. We know that the writing over the entrance says, "Abandon all hope, ye who enter here." We know they will eventually be wheeled into God's waiting room where doctors, nurses, and clergy will hover over them, and pray. We ask ourselves if there is any hope for the future? It may even cross our mind; *why not end my life now?* Here's the short answer why not: we are not growing older to die, but to live.

In the following pages, we will examine the spiritual challenges of growing older. We will learn how being a senior saint puts us into a special category in God's heart. We will examine how the Protestant church came to neglect its senior saints. For the purpose of this book I have combined the various branches of Protestant Christianity into one "church" in order to simplify my presentation.

Along the way, we'll learn where Jesus is found during our old age. We'll examine ways to deal with our suffering, and why suffering is not to be feared. Finally, we'll discover the sacred mission that God has for us as his senior saints, and a pathway to experience the deeper grace that God offers us in old age.

Don't expect the usual sermon of sweetness and light. Be prepared for a piercing examination of the spiritual questions, emotional changes, and quiet suffering that awaits all of us, as we get older. And be ready to learn new ways to deal with them.

Ultimately, *Growing Older with God* is intended to provide new ways of thinking at a time when you may feel old, tired, discouraged, disenchanted, or even of ending your life.

"Most certainly I tell you, when you were young, you dressed yourself, and walked where you wanted to. But when you are old, you will stretch out your hands, and another will dress you, and carry you where you don't want to go."

~ John 21:18

PART ONE

GROWING DOUBTFUL

"Instruct a wise man, and he will be still wiser. Teach a righteous man, and he will increase in learning." ~ Proverbs 9:9

Some years ago, I came across a quote by Billy Graham, who said, "All my life I've been taught how to die, but no one ever taught me how to grow old."[1] At first, I wondered what he meant. Hundreds of books have been written about aging. Countless psychological studies have been done. Thousands of non-profit organizations have provided advice on physical issues. The Government spends millions on geriatric research. Hadn't Billy taken advantage of the mountains of information available to prepare him for life during his golden years?

Of course he had. But an aging Christian can never find spiritual answers for growing old among practitioners concerned with healing the body and mind. The finest surgeon can only save us for another day by cutting our flesh. The brightest psychiatrist can only provide a theory about the workings of our mind. The smartest chemist can only dispense hope in a little blue pill. None of them can give us a cure for the spiritual torments that attack our soul in old age. For that, we will need something stronger than a little blue pill, a scalpel or a lofty theory. We will need divine power.

A hundred and fifty years ago the evangelist Dwight L. Moody realized this when he wrote, "Preparation for old age should begin

---

[1] © 2016 Billy Graham Evangelistic Association, used with permission. All rights reserved.

no later than one's teens. A life which is empty of purpose until sixty-five will not suddenly become filled on retirement." But you will rarely find a church focused on helping people grow old. Mostly you'll find congregations that spend enormous time, money and resources focused on teaching children, and young adults how to have a prosperous life filled with high self-esteem, a wonderful marriage, greater sexual compatibility, improved financial security, and a better family life.

Given the modern church's fascination with the here-and-now, it's not surprising that its ministers don't talk about the here-and-later. Perhaps that's why many people are startled by the spiritual struggles they encounter in maturity. Their pastors didn't prepare them for it. Their church never taught them about it. Their small groups never discussed it. As they grew older they found themselves alone trying to deal with the formidable spiritual shifts caused by the distress of aging.

Why were they left to fend for themselves?

Q's

1. In what ways has your church prepared you to grow old?
2. What have you done besides making a will, trust, or savings account to prepare for old age?
3. How has your church addressed your spiritual needs as an older person?
4. Do you think Dr. Graham's observation was correct?

"To the assembly of God which is at Corinth; those who are sanctified in Christ Jesus called to be saints, with all who call on the name of our Lord Jesus Christ in every place, both theirs and ours: Grace to you and peace from God our Father and the Lord Jesus Christ. - 1 Corinthians 1:2

I'M NO SAINT

It's amazing how many Protestants don't think they're a saint. They will call themselves a child of God, citizen of the kingdom, member of the body, brother, sister, deacon, elder, disciple, or even a priest in the hood of the believers; but rarely a saint. Why is this?

It's mostly because the leaders of the Protestant Reformation believed that by being baptized, a person instantly became a member of the priesthood of believers, which placed them in direct connection with God. So, there was no need for a special class of Christian called a "saint" to serve as an inspiration for moral living, or offer intermediary prayer to God.

Many theologians condemned the belief that a saint had any special powers, or a unique connection with God as blasphemous. "Saint" was just a biblical title given to anyone who was enrolled in the church, like "student" is the academic title given to anyone enrolled in a school. With the erasure of the special meaning of the word "saint," there was no longer a reason for people to aspire to become one.

When the Protestants divided the world into two spiritual

categories, the saint, and the sinner, the word "saint" became synonymous with the word "saved." With the meaning of saint watered down to a rather unimportant title, developing models of sainthood, or programs of spiritual development for people to strive to be a saint was not a priority. Naturally, churches encouraged all saints to lead moral and virtuous lives, but there was no longer an elevated status called a "saint."

Yet despite their rejection of all things Roman Catholic, Protestants have always elevated certain Christian ministers, leaders, and academics to the status of "saint." While they may not officially call their all-stars "Saint Luther," "Saint Spurgeon," "Saint Wesley," "Saint Calvin," etc., that is exactly how they are treated.

They are venerated for their remarkable insights, they are quoted in Sunday sermons, their lives are documented in films, seminaries discuss their works, churches and children are named for them, statues are carved, busts are molded, stained glass windows are made, and some are used as models of proper Christian living.

Do Protestants ask dead saints to pray for them? No, but they ask living ones to. It's no secret that the great saints of today are routinely requested to offer invocations and benedictions at national ceremonies. They are urged to call down God's blessing in holy prayer on behalf of some special cause, or some special someone, as if their prayers have more power than yours or mine. Maybe they do. They are asked to consult with presidents and dignitaries, and give their religious insights. They provide television interviews to explain their holy beliefs, and people tune in to learn things about God.

The masses flock to stadiums, and auditoriums to hear them speak, and people pay exorbitant sums to spend time with them on a cruise ship, or at a conference to see them. So when Protestants say that there is no special status in the family of God called a venerated "saint," they are fooling themselves

In their move away from the importance of sainthood, Protestant churches lessened the identity, importance, obligations, and way of being a saint. Instead, they elevated the identity, importance, obligations, and way of being a disciple, which is something all together different. A disciple is a follower who is primarily engaged in spreading the teachings of their master. A saint is primarily engaged in leading a holy and righteous life pleasing to Jesus. Both aspects are necessary to form a comprehensive Christian character.

If a church ignores the special grace and connection to God found in the elevated standing of sainthood, everyone is pressured to do the works of a disciple such as sharing the evangelical gospel with strangers, going on mission trips, or "witnessing" at their workplace. While discipleship may fulfill one aspect of the great commission, it forgets another. Here is the other. "Be holy; for I am holy."[2]

Being a saint is about being holy, not in how many souls we can save through work. It is about saving souls through indirect methods such as contemplation, meditation, prayer, and fasting. It is practiced with the conviction that a saint can grow in their status. Sort of like how a student can grow to become a scholar, and then a professor.

---

[2] Leviticus 11:44

If sainthood isn't defined, modeled, taught, and expressed in the daily attitudes and activities of our church, we are yoked to never ending activities designed to express our spiritual value through kingdom work, tithing, and the practice of *moral virtue.* A saint is yoked to an ongoing life of devotion, composure, and contact with the Holy Spirit leading to a practice of *intellectual virtue.*

The difference should be apparent; a disciple does the tangible work of God's Body using temporal means, and a saint does the holy work of God's Spirit using intangible methods. When combined, they shape a balanced believer who lives a life of moral and intellectual virtue that keeps them from being "conformed to this world," and helps them to be, "transformed by the renewing of [their] mind, so that [they] may prove what is the good, well-pleasing, and the perfect will of God." [3]

The title of saint is conferred at our baptism when we enter into the family of God. But simply being immersed in the baptismal water is not enough to show our conviction. We must live the life of a saint. We will have to endure the trials of the vocation we have chosen. In the case of our baptism, God asks his saints to partner with him in a covenant of self-discipline and self-sacrifice, "Gather my saints together to me, those who have made a covenant with me by sacrifice."[4]

It should come as no surprise then, that God's saints are singled out in the scriptures, not his disciples. We do not read that God

---

[3] Romans 12:2

[4] Psalm 50:5

mourns the death of his disciples, but his saints.[5] Paul does not call the members of the church in Jerusalem and elsewhere, disciples, but saints. In the Book of Revelation, Saint John does not depict the body of Christ as an assembly of disciples, but of saints who "keep the commandments of God, and the faith of Jesus."[6] What does this mean? Simply this. Old age is the perfect time to slow down our work as a disciple, and speed up our work as a saint. But we must be taught how.

Q's

1. What is the difference between being a disciple, and being a saint?
2. Is sainthood defined by your moral and ethical decisions, or something different?
3. Where in the Bible will you find saints mentioned?
4. In what ways can you practice the life of a saint at any age?
5. Can a person be a saint, and a sinner at the same time?

---

[5] Psalm 116:15

[6] Revelation 14:2

"As for the saints who are in the earth, they are the excellent ones in whom is all my delight." - Psalm 16:3

THE SAINT EMERITUS

In my attempt to emphasize the special status of a Christian blessed with long life, I coined a title: The Saint Emeritus. Saint, for who we are as baptized Christians, and Emeritus for our lifelong contributions as a disciple. But at what point did we become a Saint Emeritus? Was it on the day we retired from work? Was it when we became an empty nester? Perhaps it was when we started collecting Social Security or Medicare?

Some people say it was the day they realized that others began treating them differently. One man told me that it was the first time he walked into a room filled with pretty women, and not one of them looked up at him. He suddenly realized that he'd become invisible, an old man no longer a part of the gene pool. A woman I know confessed that she knew the moment she saw the flabby folds under her arms. Another admitted that it was when the waitress said, "I've already applied your senior discount to the bill." For most of us, it's the day the doctor hands us the results of a test and says we have a little problem.

My time came when I was fifty-seven years old. I had just returned from back-to-back deployments to Iraq. During the two years I'd spent in combat, more than five hundred soldiers had been killed. I had officiated, supervised or attended most of their memorial services. I was exhausted, and depressed.

One day, while having coffee with a friend who was an Army surgeon, I told him that I was wrung out. He asked me when was the last time I'd taken a physical examination? I couldn't remember. Maybe when I was eighteen? Like most hard chargers, I'd avoided the stigma of the medical clinic during my career. But at his urging, I made an appointment. What could possibly be wrong? I'd always been in perfect heath. I was still parachuting out of aircraft, and traveling around the battlefield in heavy body armor well into my fifties. I felt great.

But one appointment turned into a dozen, and for the next two years I was in and out of military hospitals for a litany of reasons. I was shocked. How could I feel so good on the outside and be such a mess on the inside? My doctor friend just laughed and said, "While you were out ministering, you got old."

Somehow while I wasn't looking, I had contracted the disease of aging. My life had passed me by, and my time on earth had been stolen while I was busy living it. Saint James laughed at me from the pages of his letter. His words stung, "For what is your life? You are but a vapor that appears for a little time, and then vanishes away." [7]

It dawned on me that I'd been living the illusion of youth for a long time. Then I thought of the millions of other men and women my age that had no idea that they were in the same condition. With most of my life behind me, and mortality looming ahead, I wondered what I was supposed to do? The corporate church of everlasting youth never spoke about growing

[7] James 4:14

old, much less of the spiritual adjustments, theological changes, and other disorders that old age brings.

Why not?

Q's

1. They say that being old is just a number. Do you believe that, or is it something more?
2. Have you realized that you are older than most people around you? If so, how did you arrive at that conclusion? Did it change you?
3. Describe the event that let you know that you were no longer young?
4. They say that the average male lifespan in the United States is 73.4, and a woman's is 80.[8] How many years do you have left?
5. Do you believe that Christians are automatically a saint? Explain.
6. Do you believe that a saint has special qualities that you can learn, and exhibit? What would they be?

---

[8] https://women-s.net/average-life-expectancy-for-women/

"You have set our iniquities before you, our secret sins in the light of your presence. For all our days have passed away in your wrath. We bring our years to an end as a sigh. The days of our years are seventy, or even by reason of strength eighty years; yet their pride is but labor and sorrow, for it passes quickly, and we fly away. Who knows the power of your anger, your wrath according to the fear that is due to you? So teach us to number our days, that we may gain a heart of wisdom." - Psalm 90:10

SPIRITUAL TRIALS OF AGING

Aging tests the human spirit during a time when we are struggling with vanished titles, vanished identities, disappearing importance, lost health, and departed youth. It's a season of unexpected fears and unanticipated feelings. Ominous sensations of defenselessness, dark moods of uselessness, and crushing moments of hopelessness can threaten to overwhelm even the most active faith. More than anything, it's a time of dreadful realization that we will be utterly alone right up to the moment of our last breath.

Whether we are the rulers of the world or the ruled, rich or poor, a man or woman, saved or unsaved, black, brown, yellow, white or red, as we grow older we all wrestle with the impact of a wrinkling face, decaying body, upside down roles, changing relationships, crazy emotional challenges and different understandings of how things must now work.

I've walked the halls of nursing homes and seen the look of confusion in the eyes of people who were once essential. I've visited rest homes where disappointed souls lived alone feeling like the discarded victims of an indifferent world. I've called on the terminally ill, who bore the look of the condemned waiting their execution. I couldn't blame them for hating their fate. Who wouldn't feel degraded needing assistance using the toilet, or humiliated getting a sponge bath from a stranger, or embarrassed being fed applesauce by a part-time assistant?

I shuddered, knowing that I would probably join them someday. I lifted up my eyes to the hills. Where would my help come from? I asked God to give strength to all of us who would eventually suffer a dwindling life that we didn't expect to end this way, a life where nothing awaited us but death.

Q's

1. What tests of aging have you undergone? What are you currently undergoing?
2. Have you ever visited a nursing home? If so, what were your impressions? Would you be content to live in one?
3. Can you afford years and years of elder care?
4. Have you had any unexpected fears or ominous sensations of defenselessness, dark moods of uselessness or crushing moments of hopelessness? If so, how did/do you deal with them?

"For I am already being offered, and the time of my departure has come. I have fought the good fight. I have finished the course. I have kept the faith. From now on, there is stored up for me the crown of righteousness, which the Lord, the righteous judge, will give to me on that day; and not to me only, but also to all those who have loved his appearing." - 2 Timothy 4:7

THERE'S A SIGNPOST UP AHEAD

In the last years of his life, Saint Paul wrote to his protégé Saint Timothy about his impending death, "The time of my departure has come. I have fought the good fight. I have finished the course." Paul's comment is intended to remind us of the day that's coming when we will all be old, tired, and weak; exhausted from a life of fighting, suffering, disappointment, and reversals. Paul's words may have a certain value for younger people, but his thoughts are sacred to those of us being slowly smothered by a lingering existence. They are golden for people who "have longed for Christ's appearing" to rescue them from the suffering and trials of old age.

Everyone over fifty should be able to resonate with Paul, who sees his looming mortality. We have a kinship with this man who calls himself, "the chief sinner."[9] We have read about his seething anger and lofty pride, and we are glad to know he is just like us.

[9] 1 Timothy 1:15

We find comfort in his religious arrogance, and his hatred for others because we see that he is no better than us. We resonate with Paul's disillusionment in religious legalism, and the folly of scholarly intellect knowing that our instincts are right. We love Paul because we see a disabled soul redeemed; a man of fury stripped of his false perceptions, and a soul divested of his worldly illusions.

Yet despite all of his sins and mistakes, he eagerly anticipates the crown of righteousness that he knows Jesus will award him at his death. But his ironclad confidence came at a high price. It did not materialize in a church conference or during a weekend retreat. Paul has struggled with detractors, been flogged in the synagogues, sacrificed his considerable identity as a Pharisee, endured prison, suffered the ongoing pain of a physical ailment, braved the wrath of nature, and was ultimately martyred by the emperor, all to bring the good news of Jesus Christ to the empire. Paul is a redeemed giant of the faith standing toe to toe with Moses and all the other old men and women of the Bible who served God as deeply flawed mortals to the end of their lives.

What does this mean to us?

It means that by documenting Paul's life and trials, God has shown us the model of behavior and commitment he expects of an older saint. And rather than making us pour through all the pages of the Old and New Testament, God uses Paul's pen to summarize his four most important expectations. 1. Be serious in all things. 2. Suffer hardship. 3. Do the work of an evangelist. 4.

And fulfill your ministry."[10] In the following pages, we will explore how we can fulfill these requirements in the final years of our life.

Q's

1. In the Bible, Paul calls himself "the chief sinner." If Paul were as bad as he says, how could he possibly be a saint or a candidate for heaven?
2. What sins of Paul do you have? Have you ever had a murderous heart? Have you ever persecuted others who didn't believe like you? Have you ever cursed? Have you ever been a violent person? Are you an arrogant person?
3. How did God transform Paul from being a fanatical disciple of a religious viewpoint, into a holy saint?
4. Are you old enough to know that your life is being poured out like a drink offering? Can you see that the day of your departure is near? If so, how are you dealing with these truths?

---

[10] 2 Timothy 4:5

"Jesus came out wearing the crown of thorns, and the purple garment. Pilate said to them, "Behold, the man!" ~ John 19:5

THE NEXT HILL

Given the many disappointments, traps, and temptations that old age brings, let's turn our attention to what it means to grow old, and wear the crown of a Saint Emeritus. It's a crown of suffering forced upon us like the one pressed down upon the head of Jesus by life's cruel executioners.

We don't want it.

Unlike the wonderment we had as a child looking forward to what's over the next hill, in old age we know what's over the next hill. We've seen the emaciated bodies of the decrepit elderly. We've helped lay our parents, and grandparents to rest. We know where this all ends.

"How did we get here?" we ask.

This is how I remember it.

Those of us called baby boomers were born last century. The writer Tom Wolfe called us the "Me Generation" as a comment upon our generation's blatant narcissism. We were the pampered children of depression era mothers and fathers who had survived a world war and were determined that their children would not be denied. Thanks to them, we experienced a different America than they did.

It was the Age of Aquarius and a time of relative safety,

confidence, and promise. Tomorrowland was Disneyland's metaphor of an exciting technological future, Detroit made whimsical cars with spaceship fins, and we believed the USA was on the side of truth in a never-ending battle against evildoers.

But then the culture started to collapse, and America experienced political unrest, social upheaval, new age religions, drugs and the unleashing of sexual pleasures. By the end of the century, the modern Christian interpretation of Saint Paul's reflection on aging became something like this:

> "For I have already poured myself a drink because the time ofmy cruise departure is near. I have fought the good social fight,I have finished the corporate race, and I have kept up the appearanceof faith. Now there is in store for me the crown of retirement, whichthe Lord, the righteous judge, will award to me on that day whenI am entitled to collect my Social Security and cash in my 401K.And not only to me, but also to all Christian's who have longedfor their investment portfolio's appearing."

Let the good times roll!

When the 2000s arrived, we were busy in our midlife working, raising families and building our nest eggs. Then the news came that those corporations too big to fail, failed, followed by some of the biggest financial disasters in U.S. history. Millions of seniors, and those soon to become seniors, lost their homes, stock investments, and savings. Many of them never recovered. It was too late to double down on the stock market or recoup their money in some other way. They were too old. They didn't have enough time left. We all woke up.

Q's

1. Describe your life growing up. What was it like for you?
2. How have the events of the past half-century impacted you physically, emotionally, spiritually?
3. Do you fear that you will outlive your money?

"How long, Yahweh? Will you forget me forever? How long will you hide your face from me?" ~ Psalm 13:1

STAYING ALIVE

The most significant issue most people face in old age is just trying to stay healthy and alive. Many seniors are flat broke, and those with a pension, social security, and stock investments have seen their buying power dwindle due to inflation, rising consumer costs, and increased tax rates. Those depending upon Social Security learned that there is no security in social security. Many discovered too late that social security is only meant to provide them a "foundation of income" from which they were expected to build on. Meaning, that they'd better find another job in their golden years. Meaning, that millions of seniors will have to work until they die. But who is hiring a sixty-five-year-old retired engineer?

"Would you like fries with that order?"

There is just no way that a senior citizen receiving Social Security can afford to live on it. Unless they have a generous retirement package or hit the mega-lotto they won't even be able to pay the average healthcare expenses projected to cost over two hundred thousand dollars spanning the ages of sixty-five to seventy-five.

Granted, some folks did well in their working years, and you see them traveling the highways in their motor homes dragging an SUV behind them. But they are the exceptions. Most older people are hopelessly struggling to make ends meet on meager earnings from a combination of a part-time job, and Social Security.

Today, sixty-two percent of all retired persons depend on Social Security for at least half of their monthly income, and about thirty-three percent rely on it for their entire income. Many of them have been surprised to learn that after a lifetime of payments into a compulsory system, the average return on their payroll investment was a paltry $1,404 dollars a month, or an annual income of $16,848. Not nearly enough to afford the monthly costs of modern senior care.

Then, imagine their astonishment when they applied for government aid and learned that Washington made sure that their Social Security payout was just enough income to make them ineligible for every Federal assistance program available to the average homeless person, illegal alien or indigent. Is it any wonder that many seniors are depressed, or in a quiet panic?

"Sure mom, we'd love for you and dad to come live with us."

Moreover, there are serious reports that the Social Security reserve will be insolvent by 2037, creating a looming disaster for future Saints Emeritus.[11] But seniors have other problems too. Take the epidemic of olders who are numbing their stress and pain with prescription opioids like OxyContin. In 2016 one third of those receiving Medicare had an opioid prescription. Many, who couldn't get a prescription, got cheaper painkillers sold on

---

[11] https://money.usnews.com/money/personal-finance/articles/2009/06/16/how-to-prepare-for-the-end-of-social-security

the streets. Worse, between 2002 and 2014, opioid abuse almost doubled among Americans over age fifty.[12]

"But I have a prescription from the doctor so it's okay."

Then there is the growing number of seniors who frequent the casinos and racetracks, praying on their knees to hit the jackpot. According to the American Gaming Association, thirty-six percent of those from the ages of fifty to sixty-four, and twenty-eight percent of people sixty-five and older visited gambling casinos in 2012.

Unsurprisingly, lots of them gambled more than they could afford. Many are losing their fixed income or retirement funds to the roulette wheel. And those who can't get to a casino can always gamble online, or through government-sponsored lotteries promoted as educational charities at any market or gas station. And don't forget the bingo and poker nights at the senior centers, lodges, and churches that legitimize gambling addiction.

If that weren't bad enough, a 2014 survey claims that thirty-six percent of seniors are victims to telemarketing and financial scammers.[13] Add the fact that more and more seniors are being duped by criminal fraud, theft by a family member, or the victims of caregiver abuse it might explain why the number of seniors committing suicide is rising.

To make matters worse, the national push to euthanize or provide physician-assisted suicide to seniors is growing. Next to the preborn, seniors are the largest group targeted for elimination by a society that

---

[12] Substance Abuse and Mental Health Services Administration

[13] True Link Financial, http://documents.truelinkfinancial.com/True-Link-Report-on-Elder-Financial-Abuse-Executive-Summary_012815.pdf

believes they are no longer productive, are a financial burden upon the healthcare system, or are going to die anyway.

During 2017 in the State of California, over five hundred people received aid-in-dying drugs. About ninety percent were older than sixty. In 2012, almost seven thousand people older than sixty-five committed assisted suicide throughout the nation.[14] And who knows how many thousands have committed "silent suicide" by merely giving up the ghost in their recliners by overdosing on narcotics, or refusing to take their medications?

In addition to all of these problems, more and more older people are becoming a part of the "sandwich generation," a term for people struggling to care and financially support their aging parents, and their children or grandchildren at the same time.

Before you say "not in my church," take a look around. The awkward truth is that plenty of little old church ladies take more than a nip or two of the cooking sherry. Lots of olders are blurry-eyed from narcotic prescriptions, and more people than you think are spending their savings to purchase scratch-off tickets or chances at the church raffle hoping to improve their lives. And never doubt for a second that the thought of painless euthanasia hasn't crossed the minds of many older people in your church who suffer from incurable chronic pain.

God only knows how many olders have reached their breaking point. No wonder they can't keep their mind focused on God while the minister drones on about the abundant life, or a mission trip to somewhere. The mission is sitting right under his nose.

---

[14] Centers for Disease Control and Prevention (CDC) Data & Statistics Fatal Injury Report for 2012.

Q's

1. What physical, emotional, spiritual, and financial hardships are you facing?
2. What is your church doing to help the older members of the congregation overcome the difficulties they confront? Are any spiritual programs offered? Any financial resources allocated?
3. Why do you think seniors are some of the most prominent advocates for self-inflicted death, and some of the major supporters of organizations who champion suicidal death?

"He also spoke a parable to them that they must always pray, and not give up." - Luke 18:1

THE STORM INSIDE

I've known older people who've prayed for death. Take the case of a man I'll call Deacon Tim. During his lifetime, Tim was a rich, important, and well-known man. He'd traveled the world, written several books, been a respected member of his profession, and had served as a Sunday school teacher at a very prestigious big steeple church. At seventy-six Tim was a relatively young man. When I met him, he'd just moved into an assisted living facility. His entire world had been reduced to a desk, bookshelf, small television, twin bed, and a tiny bathroom just big enough to turn around in. Since the passing of his wife, he'd been living with his children until the diagnosis of a terminal disease caused them to relocate him to a place they thought could better manage his care.

When I knocked on his door, I was prepared to find an unhappy man. But what I found was an inconsolable man. Nothing I could say or pray changed his attitude or outlook. He was mad at God, seething with resentment at his situation, fuming with anger at his children, and had a deep-seated fear that his past sins in life would damn him to hell by some imaginary force.

Tim was a tormented Christian who repeatedly mourned that God had been unfair to him. He sobbed that there was no reason to live. I prayed, he prayed, everybody prayed yet nothing helped him. Less than a week later Tim went to his grave, a pitiful man of fury who suffered alone in a room that smelled faintly of disinfectant. I wondered how a man could spend his entire life as a Christian and end up like this.

I thought of Dr. Viktor Frankel, a clinical psychiatrist, and Holocaust survivor whose book; "Man's Search for Meaning" provides the world with a first-hand observation of life in a concentration camp. He wrote that people who'd lost their meaning and purpose could become so discouraged that they simply gave up living and willed their own death.

Had Deacon Tim lost his meaning? Had he given up the desire to live? If so, why? Isn't the highest joy of a Christian to know that they have hope in Jesus during this life and beyond? I was puzzled. Had the church somehow failed Tim? Hadn't all the sermons on how much Jesus loved him been enough to sustain him?

Before you say, "he must not have been a Christian," take the story of a man I'll call Pastor Jackson. He'd been a popular executive pastor of a large church who'd served his congregation faithfully for more than twenty-five years. After retirement, he dabbled in part-time ministry and volunteered with various charity organizations. Some months later, he received the bad news that he had brain cancer. As if an internal light-switch had been flipped, his countenance darkened and overnight he fell to pieces. The once well-spoken, smooth and gracious man collapsed into a pathetic spiritual wreck. Like Deacon Tim, he railed against the very God he had served. He wrung his hands in anguish and lashed out at both his family and friends. Time went by, but nothing could bring back the pleasant personality of this learned servant of God. Again, I watched another Christian man give up and die broken and indignant.

Finally, there was a woman I'll call Ms. Joan, who at the age of eighty-five, had outlived her husband and all of her friends. She lived alone, refusing to move into a nursing home because she feared that they would take advantage of her. Her mind was sharp, but her mobility had become a major issue. Nevertheless, she was still able to feed herself, and with a visit from a caregiver every day she could meet her personal needs.

Several falls had resulted in unrelenting neck and back pain that medications couldn't help. High blood pressure, heart issues, and a variety of organ problems had resulted in a coffee table stacked high with medicine bottles. She sat by herself all day long with a blaring television her only companion. She was a lifelong churchgoer until she became too fragile to attend anymore.

She told me that she prayed every day for God to let her die. She said she had no life, no purpose, and her pain was unbearable. She couldn't understand why God would allow her torment to go on. She'd been faithful, she'd fought the good fight, but now there was nothing more to do, no place to go, and no hope for anything better. More than once she confided, "Don't pray for me to get better. Pray for me to die soon."

I wondered how these three Christians who had attended church all their lives, and served in numerous church positions could finish this way? Something was desperately wrong. How could they reach the end of their lives in such a state of spiritual hopelessness? Even more puzzling was that in all three of their cases their spirit seemed to die long before their body did. And please don't think these are isolated examples. I could relate many more stories of older Christians who have not finished well.

I am told that it's disrespectful to suggest that their church had any role in their broken ending. I am advised that it is rude to ask why so many baptized Christians give up when confronted by the tsunami of suffering that aging brings them. I am cautioned that it is audacious to mention the number of pastors, elders and deacons who have committed suicide.

Nevertheless, it is fair to ask legitimate questions about the spiritual condition of our senior citizens in an age where modern medicine extends the years of our lives, but not necessarily the quality. We have the responsibility to examine what drove Christians like Deacon Tim, Pastor Jackson, and Ms. Joan to their bitterness, or desperation.

Right now, there are many older Christians who are suffering quietly, spiritually troubled, some even thinking about committing suicide in your community. Isn't it time that churches examine their educational programs to determine if new curriculums can be written to accommodate the spiritual needs of people face the trials of old age? At the very least the church should examine why any Christian could ever die without feeling they have a meaning, purpose or any hope except for death to take them.

Q's

1. Is there anything that would convince you to take your own life? Explain why or why not.
2. Have you ever known someone who has committed suicide? How did you feel about that?
3. What do you believe God thinks about suicide? Does he punish us if we do? Does he care?
4. Why do you think Deacon Tim, Pastor Jackson, and Ms. Joan became disheartened? Have you ever felt ready to give up?

"You have taken my friends from me. You have made me an abomination to them. I am confined, and I can't escape." ~ Psalm 88:8

THE INEVITABLE

Naturally not every older Christian commits suicide, or dies in whimpering rage. But the realization of having to live a long drawn out existence of monotonous hospital trips, painful treatments, and growing isolation from family and friends can cause anxiety in even the strongest soul. The perceived injustice of being trapped in a body that no longer responds to their commands in a world that no longer responds to them can be overpowering.

Preachers rarely make of point of telling their congregation that almost everyone will end up facing these challenges. They know better than to make an issue about suffering, dying, and death. People don't like hearing about such things. They might not come back next Sunday. Topics relevant to the senior experience such as grief, night terrors, anxiety, solitude, public debasement, paranoia, depression, bullying, and personal humiliation are not big draws for people seeking the abundant life.

So the religious empathy industry presents warm edifying lectures containing charming stories, sports illustrations, and folksy humor presented with cool guitar riffs, and digital piano licks meant to sell the great, excellent, virtuous, kindly, agreeable, friendly, pleasant, exciting news of a sentimental God who lives to shower his children with good health, a wonderful family life, financial happiness, and all the comfort they deserve.

And all God's people said, "Tell us another bedtime story pastor; the kind with rainbows, sunshine, and showers of blessings."

No wonder so many elderly Christians are unhappy when they hit the wall, and church fellowship, rituals, rites, doctrines, and bouncy leadership don't overcome their spiritual problems. That's when they begin to ask, "Where's the joy being stuck in a wheelchair, paralyzed by a stroke, and drooling spit down the side of my mouth? Where is the God of prosperity and abundance in all of this?"

Today's church doesn't specialize in the spiritual changes found in old age. That's not to say that they won't continue to serve as God's cheerleaders to keep our morale high. But the pulpit of divine comfort doesn't offer old people the kind of spiritual leadership that is relevant to their new situation in life.

Q's

1. How has your church trained you to cope with the spiritual changes that aging eventually brings?
2. What table talks or programs have been offered to provide you with ways to handle the apprehensions of growing older?
3. Do you have any fears about aging?

"Don't say, 'Why were the former days better than these?' For you do not ask wisely about this." ~ Eccl. 7:10

LOOKING BACKWARD GOING FORWARD

One thing that keeps us from having a positive attitude, as we grow older is that we love to look back on our life with nostalgia. Longing for the past generally begins when we are old enough to have a history long enough to long for; which I think is about fifty or sixty years of age.

The main street in my town is lined with antique stores where I sometimes browse among the dusty relics of the past. A James Bond movie poster, 1968 World Series baseball program, or a Lionel Train can bring back sweet memories of childhood. There's nothing wrong with a bit of nostalgia. But what of those older people who are lost in the past and never leave the 60s, 70s or age of disco?

Do you know anyone who relates for the umpteenth time that glorious moment back in high school when they made the clutch play that won the game that sent the team to the State championships? Have you ever met a person who regularly talks about the music back then, the styles they wore or the great television shows of the time? Do you have any friends who reminisce about old romantic partners, look forward to their class reunion, haunt classic car shows, attend nostalgia rock concerts, or participate in any activity designed to transport them back to another time?

Sigh, such happy days.

Let's examine the problem of nostalgia by dividing our lives into three phases. In the first phase, we are youngsters anxiously preparing for the time when we will be grown up. The second phase is when we are grown-up and busy with the tasks of raising a family, earning a living, or improving our career. In the final phase, we are turning into older people. We are about as settled and grown up as we are ever going to get. In other words, there is more of our life behind us than before us. This is the phase where it becomes tempting to slip into a neurotic yearning for an earlier time when our identity seemed to be at its height, and everything appeared to be bright and cheery.

But the danger in reminiscing is that we will not see our past for what it really was, or that we will unconsciously embellish our achievements, possessions, and associations to the point that they become mental idols we turn to for comfort. The risk is that if we become hooked on illusions of the past, there is a real potential to create an unhealthy self-discontinuity that can destroy our ability to enjoy the present, and our capacity to function as healthy souls.

The ancient Greeks recognized the trap when they combined the word *nostos,* meaning return, with *algos,* meaning suffering. When put together, they create a word that represents self-inflicted pain caused by a yearn to return, nostalgia.

Besides, when we gaze into the past we become like sailors trying to row a boat forward by looking backward. Maybe this is why so many older people get depressed. Perhaps they are tired of zigzagging back and forth through the sea of life always looking backwards in nostalgia. When I was in the Army, we used to say,

God only gives you a certain number of heartbeats; so don't waste them jogging. Today I say, God only gives you so many minutes of life; so don't waste them looking backward.

One of the major teaching points of the Bible is that God expects his people to always move forward towards something more significant that he has planned. In the Old Testament, Yahweh says to Moses, "Speak to the children of Israel, that they go forward."[15] Later, he taught the Hebrews a bitter lesson when they kept looking backward to the land of Egypt with a nostalgic love for their former life. "Yahweh sent fiery serpents among the people, and they bit the people; and many people of Israel died."[16] The lesson is that God's people must always look forward to what he has in store for them, and never linger in the past.

Still, you may wonder how a bit of harmless nostalgia can be dangerous to your life? So, let's examine this passage from the story of the destruction of Sodom and Gomorrah. "When the morning came, the angels hurried Lot saying, "Get up! Take your wife, and your two daughters, lest you be consumed in the iniquity of the city . . . Escape for your life! Don't look behind you, and don't stay anywhere in the plain. Escape to the mountains, lest you be consumed! But Lot's wife looked back, and she became a pillar of salt."[17]

The Old Testament phrase "to look back" means more than to just take a simple glance, it means to dwell upon or deeply consider. Could it be that Lot's wife looked back in nostalgia and

---

[15] Exodus 14:15

[16] Numbers 21:6

[17] Genesis. 19:26

was so overwhelmed at the thought of leaving her past life that it paralyzed her? Was she unable to say goodbye to everything she knew. Did it result in the death of her soul?

In her defense, perhaps she had wonderful memories of growing up in the community of Sodom, where she married Lot, raised their children, enjoyed the social acceptance of others, and received the comfort of her close friends. Perhaps, but when she looked back with more than just a casual interest, she placed her identity in a past that she was told must be destroyed. When she turned away from the direction that the angels pointed, she committed spiritual suicide. The Bible tells us the result was that this unnamed woman turned into a pillar of salt, which is an object that is both immovable and poisonous.

We are commanded to leave our imaginary world behind, and move forward towards the "mountains" of the Promised Land. The fate of Lot's wife is a lesson for what happens when we do not obey. It is the end for those who cannot tear themselves away from their past. The sooner we tear down our precious memory shrines, the easier it is to grow older with God.

Admittedly, as sinners, we will always be tempted to look back and seek refuge or comfort in the memories of the past. But the angels still order, "Escape for your life! Don't look behind you, and don't stay anywhere in the plain. Escape to the mountains, lest you be consumed!"[18]

What will you do?

---

[18] Genesis 19:17

Q's

1. In what ways are you still tied to the past?
2. Have nostalgic trips down memory lane ever brought you self-inflicted sadness?
3. The angels warned Lot, "Escape for your life! Don't look behind you, and don't stay anywhere in the plain. Escape to the mountains." What do you think they meant? How can we escape today? What does "the plain mean," and where are "the mountains?"

"For godly sorrow works repentance to salvation, which brings no regret. But the sorrow of the world works death."
~ 2 Corinthians 7:10

THE FIENDISH FAMILY

Nostalgia is married to regret. Together they spawn the evil twins of melancholy and misery. Whenever we look back on our life, we invite this unholy family to pay us a visit.

I remember a guy who loved telling the story about driving his '70 Chevy SS convertible down the Pacific Coast Highway back in high school with his girlfriend at his side. "I loved that car," he'd say. And then he'd add, "I was stupid to sell it, it would have been worth a fortune by now." When asked what happened to the girl, he'd get a sad look, and then frown. "I broke up with her. It was another stupid decision." Which begs the question, why is it that most of our pleasant memories are somehow instantly ruined by a sense of regret?

The Bible tells us that there are two types of regret. The first is a regret that brings "godly sorrow," which moves us to genuine repentance leading to a personal salvation experience.[19] Some people call this moment being "born again." The Bible then says that once we've experienced this salvation, we have no further need to look back again. "For godly sorrow works repentance to

---

[19] Corinthians 7:10

salvation, which brings no [more] regret."[20]

Then there is a second type of regret called the "sorrow of the world," which is all of the minor regrets in our life that we keep rehashing for no good reason. When we wallow in the sorrow of our minor regrets, it can lead us into neurotic behavior, clinical depression, over medication, and worse. And, as if to underscore the danger of continually mulling over our regrets, Saint Paul warns, "The sorrow of the world works death."[21]

When a Christian waxes nostalgic and thereby dredges up regret, they invite an unhealthy self-condemnation that hamstrings the work of God's grace. They inadvertently question the wisdom of Jesus who, for his purposes, allowed them to make past mistakes.

But how can we overcome the sorrowful regrets of our past?

In Saint Paul's letter to the Philippians, he tells us that despite his weakness, he was able to overcome his regrets by deliberately forgetting the past. No easy task. But this is how he says he did it. "Brothers, I don't regard myself as yet having taken hold, but one thing I do. Forgetting the things which are behind, and stretching forward to the things which are before, I press on toward the goal for the prize of the high calling of God in Christ Jesus."[22]

In this short instruction, he lays out the steps we can follow to leave the past in the past. Drawing upon Yahweh's Old Testament command to "go forward," Paul says that he stretches forward towards the things of tomorrow. Meaning that he has deliberately

---

[20] 2 Corinthians 7:10

[21] 2 Corinthians 7:10

[22] Philippians 3:13

stopped looking backward at his life because he knows it can surface paralyzing regrets. What you ask could Paul ever regret? How about being an accomplice to Stephen's murder, and his arrogant persecution of innocent Christians living in Jerusalem?

But Paul asked God's forgiveness for his past sins, believed in God's forgiveness, and got up every day with the determination to focus on looking forward to the goal of the prize that awaited him as a servant of the high calling of God in Jesus Christ. In other words, no more looking back.

If you've experienced the godly regret that brings repentance leading to your salvation, realize that you have no more reason to regret. By rehashing the minor regrets of your life you will bring nothing but the sorrow of the world upon your soul that will hamper your efforts to focus on the goal of obtaining the prize of the high calling of God in Jesus Christ. Stop dredging up memories that will lead to sorrowful regret. Then, write this on the blackboard one hundred times,

"Regret brings the sorrow of the world that works my death."

Q's

1. Do you believe that you are a servant of the high calling of God? Does God have a prize waiting for you at the end of your life?
2. Has God forgiven you? Or do you feel that the mistakes of your past will weigh against you on Judgment Day?

3. Do you believe that God wants to help you stop regretting past mistakes? Write down the regrets you want God to help you forget.
4. What can you do whenever you feel the urge to linger on a memory?
5. Describe a method that you think Saint Paul might have used to forget the things that were behind him, and to press forward on the things that were before him?

"For in the multitude of dreams there are vanities, as well as in many words: but you must fear God." ~ Eccl 5:7

FADING DREAMS

One of the hardest things for us to sacrifice is our worldly dreams for success, recognition, power, or some other goal. They are manufactured in our minds and have sustained us, propelled us forward, and provided us with a sense of accomplishment when fulfilled. But our worldly dreams are not the only kind of dream we can experience. There are other dreams that we don't manufacture.

1. Sleeping dreams come when we are slumbering. We have no control over their content as they pass through our minds.

2. Supernatural dreams are those where the voice of God, or his angel literally speak to us in our sleep. The Bible tells us, "God speaks once, yes twice, though man pays no attention. In a dream, in a vision of the night, when deep sleep falls on men, in slumbering on the bed; then he opens the ears of men, and seals their instruction."[23] As examples, God spoke directly to Abimelech, Jacob, Laban, Solomon, the Magi, and Joseph in a supernatural dream.

---

[23] Job 33:14-17

3. Prophetic dreams are those where God does not speak directly to the individual, but they foretell a future event with such perfect accuracy that we know they must have come from God. Examples are those dreams experienced by Joseph son of Israel, Egypt's Pharaoh, Gideon's soldier, and King Nebuchadnezzar.

Our worldly dreams are those born from our inner desire for success, fame, money, power, or some other deep psychological need. We call them dreams, but they are not. They are the hopes and wishes we want to accomplish. Unlike dreams with supernatural contact or prophetic meaning, our worldly dreams are a personal hope for something to occur. We need worldly dreams to help motivate and encourage us to triumph over our fears, and seize a purpose and meaning in life.

The problem with worldly dreams is that when we finally do accomplish them, the risk is that we will dream up another worldly dream, and then our life turns into a perpetual chasing after more, and more worldly dreams. The prophet Isaiah illustrated the spiritual emptiness that can occur. "It will be like when a hungry man dreams, and behold, he eats; but he awakes, and his hunger isn't satisfied; or like when a thirsty man dreams, and behold, he drinks; but he awakes, and behold, he is faint, and he is still thirsty."[24]

When it comes to worldly dreams, we're all happy to hear the good news about the eighty-year-old woman who accomplished her dream of graduating college. Good for her we say. And of the

---

[24] Isaiah 29:8

seventy-five-year-old man who finished a Triathlon. Hooray for him. But what do they have to do with us? We've barely the strength to load our car with groceries, or heft a laundry basket into our washing machine. Our body is telling us that we will never climb a mountain again. Our mind says we are no longer as mentally swift as we once were. And we quietly grieve realizing that we have so many worldly dreams that will never be accomplished.

But why are we grieving? What is so important about our dreams other than to provide us with something to occupy our time? In the end, all of the energy, time, money, resources, concentration, and effort to make them come true are all just chasing our vanity. As wise old King Solomon pointed out, "I have seen all the works that are done under the sun; and behold, all is vanity and a chasing after wind."[25]

Before we press on, there is another kind of dream that must be mentioned. This dream has nothing to do with worldly success, fame, or power. It is not a prophetic dream or a dream containing the voice of God. It is a secret dream we keep close to our heart that we know can never come true, but we wish it would.

It's not a dream to change a past regret; it's a dream to make something right that can never be made right. It's a dream to change something we had no control over, but ended in irreversible heartbreak. It is the dream of changing a sequence of events so that the drunk driver who killed our child had taken a right turn instead of a left. Or a dream that someone we loved had not been working in the Twin Towers on September 11, 2001,

---

[25] Ecclesiastes 1:14

or a dream that we had been born with both legs.

For those who harbor a secret dream, God will answer your dream when he undoes all the wrong, and makes all things right. I don't know how he will do it, but he promises that in the kingdom coming reunions with loved ones will occur, unexplainable tragedies will be explained, suffering will be forgotten, bodies will be made whole, and our deepest dreams for soulful comfort will come true. In a kingdom that is not of this world, the dreams of this world will dissolve into nonexistence. Only the perfect dreams of God will remain.

The Apostle John bore witness to this truth saying, "I heard a loud voice out of heaven saying, "Behold, God's dwelling is with people . . . He will wipe away from them every tear from their eyes. Death will be no more; neither will there be mourning, nor crying, nor pain, any more. The first things have passed away."[26]

The world tells us that it's never too late to chase a worldly dream, which is true, unless we are chasing the wrong dream. In old age, we will need to find a dream that can last us for all eternity. We must ask what is God's dream for us?

I'm not sure what your worldly dreams have been, or what worldly dreams you are still chasing, but now is the time to set them aside, and ask Jesus to give you a dream about his perfect dream. God says, "I will pour out my Spirit on all flesh, and your sons and your daughters will prophesy. Your old men will dream dreams."[27]

Are you ready to dream a different dream?

---

[26] Revelations 21: 2-4

[27] Joel 2:28

Q's

1. The scripture says, "old men will dream dreams." What do you think older men and women will dream about?
2. Have you asked God to give you a new dream for the future? Do you think he will respond?
3. Have your dreams for power, glory, achievement, or fame changed since you were younger?
4. Do you dream in your sleep? In what ways have your night dreams changed?
5. Do you have secret dreams that are so painful that you cannot share them? Do you think God knows about them? Do you believe he will take away your sadness?
6. Do you think that Jesus has dreams? Can you imagine what they would they be? Can you describe them?

"Behold, I tell you a mystery. We will not all sleep, but we will all be changed, in a moment, in the twinkling of an eye, at the last trumpet. For the trumpet will sound, and the dead will be raised incorruptible, and we will be changed." ~ 1 Corinthians 15:51-52

TRANSFORMATIONAL GRIEF

All this brings us to the day when we are finally able to release our worldly dreams of sex, drugs, and rock n' roll and accept that our past is past. Only then can we begin the serious process of dying. That is, if we define dying as ceasing to be the person who we were just a few moments ago to become the person we are right now.

The ancient church compared the incremental process of death to that of a creature that starts as an egg, which slowly dies to become a larva, which slowly dies to become a caterpillar, which slowly dies in its chrysalis to emerge as a new creature, the butterfly.[28] Our life during old age is comparable to the suffering phase of the caterpillar struggling to break free of its chrysalis.

From the moment of our birth we have been slowly dying to the past, and moving forward into the present while anticipating the future. At each step we have undergone many incremental changes. During the process, we have been spiritually impacted with mild grief as we've watched our world, our friends, and our

[28] 1 Corinthians 15:52b

family pass away into scrapbooks, and fading memories. Our grief is especially felt the moment we realize that it is *we* who are the ones fading away into the pages of someone else's scrapbook. The poet John Donne warned us, "Therefore, ask not to know for whom the [funeral] bell tolls. It tolls for thee."[29]

When the insight finally comes that the bell is tolling for us, it can bring sadness thinking about our imminent departure. It can be depressing to watch our lives being poured out like Saint Paul's drink offering. Yet Paul seems excited about it, not depressed. Why aren't we excited?

In 1969, the Swiss-American psychiatrist Elisabeth Kubler-Ross presented a model of how people cope with death and dying. It is called the five stages of grief consisting of denial, anger, bargaining, depression, and acceptance. Kubler-Ross noted that her listing was not necessarily the order in which people experienced them, and that they could each be experienced wholly isolated from one another, and more than one could be felt at the same time. Her theory was that these five categories represented the typical mixture of reactions that people felt in their attempt to deal with loss.

That being said, I have taken her five stages of grief, and loosely correlated them to the last decades of our life, which I believe are the general periods when we are most aware that death is sneaking up on us.

---

[29] Devotions Upon Emergent Occasions, Meditation XVII; John Donne.

- From the ages of forty to fifty, *denial.* At this point, we have an understanding that someday we will die, but death seems so far into the future that we don't think about it. Sermons about death are received as academic lessons or theological abstracts about becoming saved, or getting others saved. We're too busy to think seriously about our own death.

- From the ages of fifty to sixty, *anger.* A sudden awaking jars us into a new understanding about our age that we don't like. It could be something like getting an invitation to our forty-year high school reunion, erectile dysfunction, menopause, waddles of skin under our chin, or realizing that our slang went out of style twenty years ago. (Bummer, dude.) No matter what it is, something occurs that makes us resentful that age has crept up on us, and now impacts the quality of our life or our self-image.

- From the ages of sixty to seventy, *bargaining.* During this period we try to bargain with father time in the hopes of resetting the clock. This can take on many forms. We can spend time and money trying to relive our youth, do all the things we never had time for when we were younger, obtain cosmetic surgery, or suddenly donate to charities and religious institutions hoping to catch up on back payments to God.

- From the ages of seventy to eighty, *depression*. A shallow blue funk invades our waking moments as we subconsciously ponder all of the miserable possibilities, and outcomes that could claim us. Thoughts of outliving our spouse, financial ruin, living as the victim of Alzheimer's, the possible abandonment by our family, etc. may overshadow our days and nights.

- From the ages of eighty to ninety, *acceptance*. We finally admit that we have no control over our death, and we become receptive, even passive to the inevitable. During this period there is a real danger that our faith will turn into fatalism as we become weakened by multiple fears and discomforts.

Of these five phases, the Bible teaches that the earlier we can come to an *acceptance* of our death's inevitability and prepare our soul for it, the faster we can build a life filled with genuine comfort, meaning, and purpose. The faster we can become like excited like Saint Paul.

Q's

1. Why don't people accept their destiny sooner so they can stop grieving and start living?
2. Have you acknowledged that you are in the process of dying? What small signs indicate that you are in the process of dying?

3. What stage of grief over the loss of your life do you think you are experiencing? How do you deal with it?
4. What is the difference between accepting our death in faith, verses fatalistically?

"If a man doesn't remain in me, he is thrown out as a branch, and is withered; and they gather them, throw them into the fire, and they are burned." ~ John 15:6

WHO'S YOUR DADDY?

Along with our dreams, the most difficult thing to sacrifice in old age is our identity. Most of us were born into an industrialized America that taught children that the primary goal in life was to know the rules of citizenship, love their country, and serve society. We were supposed to be productive, have a successful career, and invest for a comfortable retirement.

To help us attain these social objectives, the government spent millions of dollars educating us in state-sanctioned assembly lines designed to provide us the information we needed to perform a trade, skill, or profession. The aim was to make us a stable member of society who could contribute to the overall welfare of the nation. From the time of our childhood, we were asked, "What do you want to be when you grow up?"[30] as if our future job determined our future identity.

Since the type of work we performed determined our pay-scale in the caste of cultural approval, massive efforts were made by parents, teachers, school counselors and a variety of private and government programs to help shape our work identity as soon as possible. Early in the process, we were sorted into specialized groups; those with the

---

[30] Until very recently, it was generally assumed that girls would accept traditional roles as mothers and housewives.

potential to go on to higher learning, those going to trade schools and those requiring special educational attention. Kids who made it to college were encouraged to declare a major field of study early in the process so that they could be properly educated for a job in the four years allotted to them. Kids identified as intellects would be allowed to progress in their education to become Masters or Doctors in a specialized occupation.

On Sundays, our corporate churches taught us that God smiled upon a virtuous and useful worker. We were told that we could build our character if we expressed our love for him and our neighbor through our labor. Here are a few of my favorite scriptures used to underscore God's blessing upon those who work, and the biblical mandate to do it.

- "And whatever you do, work heartily, as for the Lord, and not for men, knowing that from the Lord you will receive the reward of the inheritance; for you serve the Lord Christ."[31]

- "Seest thou a man diligent in his business? He shall stand before kings"[32]

- "Poor is he who works with a negligent hand, but the hand of the diligent makes rich."[33]

---

[31] Colossians 3:23

[32] Proverbs 22:29

[33] Proverbs 10:4

- "The craving of a sluggard will be the death of him, because his hands refuse to work."[34]

There is an excellent reason why it's called the Protestant work ethic.

Eventually, we entered the workplace where, for the next thirty years, we labored as a productive member of society like an engineer, soldier, accountant, actor, pastor, government worker, and so forth. When people asked us who we were, we proudly told them what we did.

Then one Friday afternoon there was an office party. They presented us with a gold watch, gave us a warm hug and showered us with accolades and praises for our many contributions to the company. The moment felt splendid. It was the accomplishment of a dream. We drove home feeling good about ourselves and sat down, breathing a sigh of relief. We'd been released from the penal colony of labor hopefully never to return. Now we could finally enjoy our life.

The next day, Saturday, was just like any other weekend. A little yard work, a trip to the store and maybe a celebratory barbecue with some friends. Sunday was no different. We were up for church, brunch with the bunch and then home to watch TV football games. But on Monday our world changed. We got up and abruptly realized that we had no place to be. Just two days earlier on Friday, we had meetings, deadlines, schedules, tasks,

---

[34] Proverbs 21:25

and rules. We were individuals with meaning and purpose. Now we were just another retired face in the crowd. For the first time in thirty or forty years, we were on our own to figure out what to do with our life.

But there were more surprises to come. Soon the ringing of our cellphone was down to a trickle. Nobody was bringing us a difficult problem to solve. Texts stop flowing. No one needed our advice. It dawned on us that we'd been replaced. Our inspired leadership was no longer required. Like a hand withdrawn from a bucket of water, it was as if we had never been there. It was depressing. We thought we had more to contribute. We thought we would be remembered. Overnight we went from being an *is* to being a *was*.

Which reminds me of a story about an Army General who was once asked when he first realized that he was retired. He responded saying it was on the Monday morning after his retirement party when he got into the backseat of his sedan, and no one was up front to drive him.

When retirement comes, it can start a time of grieving over the loss of our identity formed by our work. It can begin a time of quiet mourning over the death of the person we once were. Many people begin a period of lackluster wandering and silent struggle to regain their former significance. They join social organizations or become involved in charities in the hopes that they are needed. They haunt lodges, airplane hangers, union halls, country clubs, alumni associations, veterans organizations, taverns, etc. where they can find kindred spirits who will call them by their previous title and hold them in some esteem.[35]

Others will keep busy playing golf, hunting, fishing, traveling, etc. seeking to catch up on all of the "quality" time they missed during their career. But eventually, most of them grow tired of amusing themselves and begin looking for a part-time job, volunteer work, or something to do to replace the structure, purpose and relevance they lost at retirement.[36]

Then there are those who don't grieve the loss of their identity at retirement, because they never retire. They go from one job to the next like a dependable draft horse pulling a corporate plow. It seems reasonable to them to keep on plowing. They are the kind of person who gets up, does the task, and goes home at night without an emotional investment in the job. Their self-identification is in being a worker, not the calling, fulfillment, meaning, position, title, or relevance of the work.

Take for example the man who begins working part-time as a kid in high school, then enlists for a job in the Navy. After four years he gets out and finds work selling pharmaceuticals which he does for twenty years. Then he "retires" for a few months, tackles all of the honey-do jobs around the house only to return to work taking a job in a warehouse for sixty hours a week, which he does

---

[35] My theory about women at retirement is different. I believe that most woman find their identity in their family and friends, not in their work. Retirement for a mother usually begins the day her youngest child leaves the nest. I suspect that even those women who have balanced a family with a successful career are more easily able to retire from their job, because they have never fully invested their complete identity into their position. Men do. We are wired differently.

[36] Again, I believe that women have their own grieving issues at the age of retirement and they deal with it in different ways.

for another twenty years. Eventually, after a few medical problems, he decides to "retire" again at the age of sixty-seven and takes a less stressful job in the garden department of a hardware store.

When asked if retirement had any impact upon his self-identity, he will rightly say he never retired. When asked what job he most identified with, he will say that they were all more or less the same. For a man or woman like this, their identity is in doing the work itself. As long as they can keep working at something, anything, they will suffer no loss of identity. They identify with being a good worker and will keep working until they no longer can. They have become akin to what Max Lucado calls a human doer.[37] What will happen to their identity when they can no longer *do* work?

It's easy to see why the powers and principalities of this world groom us from early childhood to place our identity in them. They have a vested interest in keeping us drudging away in their factories and office buildings wearing their corporate logos, hats, and jackets to signify our allegiance as we toil away our souls on their behalf.

Many corporate churches want us to do the same thing. They ask us to wear their hats, and tee shirts as a sign that we have placed our identity into their vision, programs, and plans.

Nevertheless, our identity should only be placed into one thing - the person called Jesus Christ. Not in being a Presbyterian, Baptist, Methodist, Episcopalian or a member of some minor, or

---

[37] Taken from, In the Grip of Grace, Max Lucado, Nelsonword Publishing Group, 1998

megachurch. The most odious identity theft takes place when black robed clergy teach people that Jesus is the church, and the church is Jesus, telling them that when they place their heart, soul and money into their church they are placing their identity into Jesus. But Jesus is a living person, not a noble concept. He is an individual, not a church, group encounter, sacred doctrine, or a religious enterprise.

Pity the unsuspecting man or woman who places their identity into their church, or their business only to end up dying with nothing but a sense of spiritual pride, and a gold plated watch. "For what does it profit a man if he gains the whole world, and loses his own self?"[38]

The over arching point is that retirement is the first time that many people experience the personal death that comes in the form of an erased identity. It is the first time that they realize something about them has been lost forever, and now they are unsure of who they are. The grieving that follows from this death can take many destructive forms.

Enlightened men and women realize that their true identity is not in the work they do, or the church they attend, but who they are in Jesus. Oddly, who they are in Jesus will be determined by the kind of work he has them do.

Sound confusing?

---

[38] Luke 9:25

Q's

1. Do you believe that work is the expression of your relevance, meaning, or purpose?
2. Did your church teach you that hard work is a way to please God?
3. Is work a form of worship?
4. In what ways are you still working?
5. To what aspects of your life have you attached your identity?
6. What do you think it means to have Jesus as your identity?

PART TWO

GROWING CLOSER

"Let us not be weary in doing good, for we will reap in due season, if we don't give up." ~ Galatians 6:9

THE ART OF DOING

The good we *do* in Jesus will be determined according to the function of grace that he gives us. According to Saint Paul, these functions of grace are called gifts. They include *prophecy* according to the proportion of our faith, *service* to the poor and others, *teaching* the fullness of God, *speaking* the words of truth, *giving* of time and wealth, *administration* of the community with care, and cheerful acts of kindness and mercy.[39]

One or more of these gifts are assigned to us by the Holy Spirit to reshape and refocus our identity in Jesus. Through the power of the Holy Spirit, these qualities are melded into one simultaneous expression of both what we *do* and who we *are* in Jesus. They provide us with a divine symmetry of outward grace (in what we do as disciples), and inward sanctity (in who we are as saints). These qualities are further enhanced with the reception of additional gifts of grace as outlined in 1 Corinthians 12:1-13, and when we pray, fast, meditate, partake of communion, worship, suffer, sacrifice and perform other outward expressions of our faith.

As I mentioned in an earlier section, being a disciple is the domain of what we do in Christ, and being a saint is the domain

---

[39] Romans 12:6

of who we are in Christ. Think of them as being like the two parts of the cross with discipleship as the vertical plank and sainthood as the horizontal. Together they intersect at the very heart of Jesus. Each is a separate expression of his love that can be learned, practiced and expressed.

However, what we *do* using the gifts of grace cannot be equated to a job or skill set. Our doing is not an act of work, but an act of Christ's love. We do not need a church to keep us doing by making breakfast tacos or managing a bake sale. We do not need to be kept doing religious things that church Elders think up for us. Doing is what we are in Jesus at all times and in all meetings. It is the expression of the gifts of grace we have been given by the Holy Spirit found our daily coming and going.

With each work of grace, our soul becomes enlarged to accept more grace. As a way of illustration, let's say our soul is like a child's balloon being inflated with helium. At first, the balloon is just a wrinkled piece of rubbery plastic laying flat on the table. But as the helium flows inside, the balloon begins to expand growing larger and after a few moments, it rises off the table into the air.

Grace is like helium filling our soul. It rounds us into three-dimensional saints and lifts us so others can see what we are doing, in and through Jesus. If we fix our identity in anything other than Jesus, we shut out the possibilities offered through the grace of the Holy Spirit. This is why many Christians remain flat, two-dimensional beings unable to rise and experience the joy of partnership with the Holy Spirit. Their identity in their church, career, or some other distraction keeps them firmly anchored to the ground.

Please don't say that you aren't strong enough, smart enough, young enough or holy enough to identify as a disciple of suffering love and a saint of grace. Jesus knows who you are and the gift of grace he wants you to be. And do not make the mistake of confusing divine grace with human courtesy or hospitality. God's grace is a sacred capability far more significant than shaking hands and patting backs at a Sunday pancake breakfast.

Q's

1. What is the difference between divine grace and human grace? How is each one carried out?
2. What gift, or gifts of grace do you believe the Holy Spirit has given you? How have they become an expression of you?
3. Could a stranger observe your gift/s of grace? How?
4. Do you think that volunteering for a secular community service organization is the best way to express the functions of grace that Saint Paul describes?

"Now there was a man of the Pharisees named Nicodemus, a ruler of the Jews. The same came to him by night, and said to him, 'Rabbi, we know that you are a teacher come from God, for no one can do these signs that you do, unless God is with him.' Jesus answered him, 'Most certainly, I tell you, unless one is born anew, he can't see the Kingdom of God.'"
~ John 3:1-3

UNLEASHING THE SCRIPTURES

When old age comes, we can wake up, open up, and grow up to find a living Savior who stands above and beyond the scriptures, or we can passively go along to get along with what others tell us about him. Most of us will continue to practice the rites, rituals, customs, language, and social habits of our church as the happy byproducts of our denomination's thinking, or our pastor's views. We will assume that we are on the right path to heaven because they say we are. However, as we grow older, a religious supremacy will not be enough to overcome the uncertainties of aging.

Dramatic shows of worship emotion, born again displays of passion, profound liturgical rites, or rituals of breast-beating piety will not be enough to soothe our soul when we struggle with an oxygen bottle. Doctrines of sage intellect will not bring us relief when our nights consist of lingering pain. Creeds of deep assurance will not provide hope when we are plugged into a dialysis machine. We will need something different, something more. We will need the touch of the living Jesus, not a religious impersonation.

Nevertheless, our church leaders will say that Jesus expects us to disciple onward supporting the team effort, group enterprise, and common cause of another important church initiative. Our commitment to God will be measured by our commitment to the great works of our church. Our level of faithfulness will be determined at the sign-up table in the foyer, and our devotion to the Great Commission will be counted in the collection plate at Sunday morning's proof of life meeting.

We may start to feel a little guilty when we can no longer become engaged, immersed, and covered by the sweat of Jesus. When old age forces us to drop behind the pack, alone, and apart from the activities of church life, we might start to secretly grow concerned. We might worry that our dedication to Christ is faltering as our medications wear us down, and medical treatments weaken our ability to attend services. We may fear that our spotty attendance will become obvious when we must stay at home to care for a spouse with Alzheimer's. But we will valiantly struggle onward.

My point is that when we get older our life changes, but the corporate church of youthful activity marches on. That is why we must stop trying to satisfy the demands of our church, and focus on the needs of our soul. It may be difficult, but we will have to reluctantly put down the burden of a disciple to find a saint's freedom found in Jesus.

But where do we find him? He is not living under the stone spires of the rich, where wealth is sacred. He does not abide in the sanctuary of the blind, where rebuke is king. He is not walking in the soundless shrine of the deaf, where convenience is adored. He is not sitting in the sanctum of the dumb, where activism rules. Nor will we find him in the chapel of the content, where satisfaction is lord.

We will have to slip away from the sacred "ologies" that have captivated us. Just as old Nicodemus did, we will have to take a daring walk outside our religious temple to discover Jesus waiting in the shadows of our preconceptions. Old age will be our last opportunity to venture beyond the limits of other people's opinions and clergy approval to experience the extraordinary miracle who is waiting for us.

Q's

1. In what ways have you gone along with the expectations of your church? Have you ever stepped outside your religious teachings like Nicodemus to find the living Jesus? If so, can you describe what it was like? What did you learn? How did it change your attitude toward the church?
2. Do you think that you have followed all of the requirements of saintly discipleship that Jesus mentions in the Gospel of Matthew, Chapters 5-7? If not, what do you think will happen to you? List his requirements that you know you can keep.
3. Has your religious life changed, as you have grown older? Have your thoughts about God changed with age?

"Be careful that you don't let anyone rob you through his philosophy and vain deceit, after the tradition of men, after the elements of the world, and not after Christ." - *Colossians 2:8*

A RENEWED FAITH

We will have to rethink our religious faith in old age. We already know what we believe. But how can we reevaluate our faith in, and through faith itself? What makes us feel like we are above being self-deceived?

Consider the following.

Faith, and belief are two separate things. Even though we often use them interchangeably, belief is actually a trust in a firmly held conviction about a temporal matter. Belief is the product of a rational conclusion based on empirical facts and data. Faith, on the other hand, is a trust in a firmly held conviction about a supernatural matter. Faith is the product of an irrational conclusion based on the complete absence of logic, data and provable facts. We may believe that our communion wafers are made of bread, because it is a verifiable truth. On the other hand, we can only have faith that they become the body of Jesus at the moment of consecration because it is an unprovable truth. As another example, the Nicene Creed is actually a statement of our faith, not beliefs. Again, we can believe that the Bible is a book, but we have a faith that it contains something sacred. The importance to this distinction is that our beliefs must be proven; our faith does not.

As outgrowths of a Western education, we've been taught to prove our beliefs about the world around us by using systems like the scientific method. The scientific method is a process of empirical investigation leading to a verifiable conclusion. In it, a problem is identified, relevant data is gathered, a theory is formulated from the collected data, and then the theory is tested to verify its accuracy.

The religious discord caused by a misunderstanding of the difference between our faith and our belief may be why we now have over two hundred different Protestant denominations in the United States,[40] all determined to prove their beliefs are correct. It may also be why churches foster a hive mentality that demands the acceptance of their corporate beliefs, not an individual personal faith.

All of this emphasis upon validating church beliefs through logical evidence has served to create a fact-based Christianity wrestling in the mud of the world's logic. What we should aspire to is a faith-based Christianity soaring above the world's understanding that brings people together instead of driving a corrosive wedge between Christians who brandish their swords of belief at each other when they are supposed to keep the unity of the *faith* in the unprovable Spirit through a bond of peace.[41]

What has happened to us? We are no longer a community of individuals sharing our personal faith revelations about the Trinity; we have become small collectives of fact checkers, and

---

[40] Association of Religious Data Archives, http://www.thearda.com

[41] Ephesians 4:3

religious research scientists trying to authenticate our personal and denominational beliefs. We have replaced the awe of God found in an intimate faith, with the awful requirement to verify our beliefs with a community that determines if we have experienced the correct understanding about God.

Authentic evangelism is meant to prove the truth of Jesus through a faith experience with him, not through a belief system of data and facts about him. All of our attempts to prove our belief in his existence in tweets of gospel facts, emails of Bible data, and webpages of intellectual evidence are a sign that we are foolishly trying to defend our unprovable faith with empirical evidence. We have never been called prove or defend our faith.[42] We have always been called to live our faith as the righteous expression of our gifts of grace.

Nevertheless, scientific thinking infects our churches, and has caused the exodus or suppression of many devoted Christians who learned that unless they were able to defend their faith with the logic of an attorney, they were challenged, dismissed or made to feel stupid by those who confused faith with belief. In churches like this, it is he with the most Bible data and facts that will rule the class, not she with the most faith.

Admittedly, it is difficult for Christians to be otherworld thinkers when all our lives we are taught worldly thinking. We have been encouraged to chase the golden ring of truth using tools

---

[42] Matthew 26:52-53 "Then Jesus said to him, "Put your sword back into its place, for all those who take the sword will die by the sword. Or do you think that I couldn't ask my Father, and he would even now send me more than twelve legions of angels?"

like the scientific method. It is how we succeed in the workplace. But success in the supernatural world is not measured by human verification, or intellectual proof systems, it is measured by faith, and faith alone.

When a church accepts the world's demand that God's Truth must be validated, it means that the congregation will never be trained in ways they need to bracket their worldly assumptions, and inner biases as they approach divine Truth. They will not be instructed in techniques of visualizing the Scriptures in a holy faith while using a sacred imagination that allows them a glimpse of the living Word standing behind the printed word. There will be no classes to teach personal introspection to help them experience their faith in the Truth who lives inside their hearts, or attempts at group intersubjectivity[43] to help them understand by faith the Truth that someone from another church says is residing in their heart.

Instead they will be handed a book, tract, or pamphlet from their religious authority telling them what to believe, and what to say to people about the literature's contents.

"Hello, I stopped by today…"

The answer to all our questions about God in our old age will not come by learning more Bible data or facts. All of the Bible knowledge, and scripture study in the world will not prove the mysteries of the Holy Trinity to us or anyone else. What we must learn is how to apprehend the Truth in a wild expression of

---

[43] Where people discuss their own experience in a circle of others about something they have experienced, and talk about how it relates to themselves and their community.

irrational, and undefendable faith. Ultimately we will all answer to the Living Truth for the character and expression of our faith, not how well we proved our religious beliefs.

Right now many of you are ripping your garments and gasping, "Ya but! Ya but!" finding it incredulous that I would criticize humanity's crowning achievement of the enlightened mind, and the universal benefits achieved through rational, reasonable, logical systems like the scientific method. I am not criticizing; I am just putting all things in their place. Using the tools of the scientific method may be appropriate in the world's workplace, but they are of no value in the new kingdom lying just over the horizon of our reason.

In the realm of God's supernatural, Truth is found by a restless spirit willing to go on a daring adventure of faith outside the walls of religious conventionalism to experience God's sacred, and suffering heart. It is discovered in a spiritual reality that exists which can sometimes be explained, and occasionally illustrated, but never proven.

If we hope to experience a more profound revelation of the Holy Spirit, it will require more than the hunt for intellectual verification within the pages of the Bible. In old age, we will need to readjust our methodology so that we can experience an illogical faith in a sometimes contradictory, completely unpredictable, and indefensible God. For that, the scientific method will not do. Nor will a first place ribbon in a Bible trivia contest. We will need to find Jesus in our inner room.

Q's

1. Have you ever tried to prove something to others about the Bible? What happened?
2. Many people dispute the Christian faith because we cannot prove that Jesus is God. Do you think that you have an obligation to prove it to them? If so, how would you do that?
3. Do you believe that people can find Jesus standing outside the "temple walls" of their religious beliefs? If so, how?
4. Does your church encourage its members to move beyond the "walls" to experience the living Jesus? In what ways do they do this?

"But you, when you pray, enter into your inner room, and having shut your door, pray to your Father who is in secret, and your Father who sees in secret will reward you openly."
- Matthew 6:6

FINDING THE INNER ROOM

How can we find Jesus living at the center of our center, the man with the power to reveal who, what, and why we are? First, we must decide that if he is really alive, we will find him. Thankfully, the Bible provides the way to the Way. Read the following scripture.

"The next day, John [the baptizer] was standing with two of his disciples, and he looked at Jesus as he walked, and said, "Behold, the Lamb of God!" The two disciples heard him speak, and they followed Jesus. Jesus turned, and saw them following, and said to them, "What are you looking for?" They said to him, "Rabbi" (which is to say, being interpreted, Teacher), "where are you staying?" He said to them, "Come, and see." They came and saw where he was staying, and they stayed with him that day."[44]

Here we see two followers of the popular evangelist John the baptizer who decided to leave his ministry and follow Jesus. As a result, Jesus acknowledged them asking what they were looking for. We'd expect them to respond, "We're looking for a life in abundance, personal prosperity, a world of comfort, safety, family

---

[44] John 1:35

protection, social justice, food for the poor, financial security, universal healthcare and healing miracles." But that's not what they wanted. Instead they asked, "Where are you staying?" Or to extend the word, "Where are you *residing*." Jesus answered them, "Come, and see." So they followed him and dwelled with Jesus the rest of the day.

You and I are like those two disciples. Except instead of following John, we follow a pastor or priest who points us to Jesus. Most of us never have the courage to leave our pastor. We do not have the same grit as the two disciples who left John in order to pursue Jesus. We are content to stay and hear our pastor's satisfying stories, or elaborate history lessons about God.

But this scripture shows us that in order for the two disciples to meet Jesus for themselves, they had to take a daring leap of faith, and leave their pastor John. Worse, they needed a persistent faith to keep them patiently following Jesus until he decided to turn and speak to them.

Their dogged persistence paid off when Jesus said, "What are you looking for?" Christians who are brave enough to leave their religious conditioning, and pursue Jesus for themselves will be asked the very same question, "What are you looking for?"

My point is that we can't meet the living God listening to the teachings of a pastor, priest or TV evangelist. He can't be found in seminary theology, religious creeds, or denominational doctrines. He must be personally experienced for the man that he is. And that requires more than just Bible study or wrapping sandwiches for the homeless. They are just the start.

Ministers and priests are like John the Baptizer; they can only speak about Jesus. But John wasn't trying to keep a church going, or growing. He wasn't trying to convince people that by listening to him they were getting closer to Jesus. John preached the radical concept that people must walk away from him to experience the truth of salvation found in a direct experience with the man whose sandal he was unworthy to touch.

As you know, Christians generally believe that the way to be saved and go to heaven is to ask Jesus into their heart and be baptized, which we all did, but then nothing much happened. No fireworks, no earthshaking revelations or mind-altering miracles. So we shrugged off the idea of ever having a divine experience with God, and settled on being a committed "person of religious faith" satisfying our church's expectations for accountability, sociability, volunteerism and financial contributions.

For many of us, as we grow older it becomes harder and harder to listen to a younger minister saying that we should be filled with joy, when we don't feel much joy. We sense that we are missing something. When they preach, "The peace of God, which surpasses all understanding will guard your hearts and your thoughts in Christ Jesus,"[45] we silently ask, *where is the peace for me?*

The problem is that in old age we must be saved again. Not from hell, but from the hell of aging. To do this, we must leave our John the Baptizer pointing to Jesus, depart the sanctuary of our comfortable stereotypes, and follow the living man, just like the two disciples did. Only then can we be invited to, "Come and see."

---

[45] Philippians 4:7

Q's

1. What answer would you give if Jesus asked you, "What are you looking for?"
2. Why would the two disciples want to know where Jesus was residing?
3. Remember Nicodemus? What did he risk by leaving the Temple to find Jesus for himself?

"One thing I have asked of Yahweh, that I will seek after, that I may dwell in the house of Yahweh all the days of my life, to see Yahweh's beauty, and to inquire in his temple."
- Psalm 27:4

COME AND SEE

How can we follow Jesus through the cloud of our unknowing to his residence? The first step will be to discover Jesus for who he really is, not what a pastor tells us. Ministers and priests are well intentioned, but we must enter Jesus' residence for ourselves. Our pastor may share their experience with Jesus, but it will never be like our own. For every hundred ministers preaching about Jesus, there are a hundred and one views on what Jesus wants of us.

Our goal is to personally dwell with Jesus so that we can know first hand his hopes, dreams, and expectations for the person he intends us to be. We do not want him filtered through the mind of a well-meaning third person. No matter what we are told, we cannot have a meaningful experience with Jesus in just a few minutes of weekly Bible study, morning devotion over coffee, an hour of groupthink, a weekend retreat, or a two-week mission trip crammed with busy church activities, forums, and planned program events.

If we want to know where Jesus resides, it will take more than a flirting attempt at immediate gratification. We will have to overcome our religious opinions, mental biases, and old work habits to journey behind him to where he resides. It will be a twisting trip of embarrassing repentance walked upon a path of cobblestones made of suffering and toil. During the journey we will pass through the dark forest of our sins. We will struggle to hack down the thick underbrush of our pretensions. We will encounter precarious switchbacks that will change our life. Every bend in the trail will reveal another shameful secret we have packed away and forgotten.

It will be difficult to look at our own soul from God's perspective. We will not want to see ourselves as he sees us. We will shrink in shame when our worldly tongue comes back to haunt us. Like the cowardly lion in the Wizard of Oz we will want to turn back. "Wait a minute, fellows. I was just thinking. I really don't want to see the Wizard this much. I'd better wait for you outside."[46]

If we wish to see where Jesus resides, it will not be a pleasant walk in the park that some ministers have promised. It will take a determined faith to follow the Way to the Way. It will take humility to step out of our religious ego, and move beyond the sacred temple of our mind to touch the hem of his robe.

If all of this seems impossible, God has provided a shortcut. It is through the blessing of old age. In our declining years he provides us with the time to know him, as we are involuntarily secluded from the distractions, amusements, and trivialities that have previously captured our attention. It is really the first time that we can focus entirely on the health of our soul.

---

[46] From the movie Wizard of Oz, 1939, Metro-Goldwyn-Mayer

When we are bedridden, we will surrender to his mercy. When a stroke impairs us, we will discover his heart in silent meditation. When we carry an oxygen bottle, we will learn to give thanks for every breath. When Parkinson's shakes our hand, we will feel his grip. When we slip into Alzheimer's, we will hear his voice speaking from inside our heart.

Strangely, the travails of old age provide a unique opportunity to follow Jesus to where he resides. You can start the journey now by saying, "Sir, I want to see Jesus."[47]

Q's

1. In what ways do you rely on others to provide you with insights into Jesus?
2. Have you ever been to where Jesus resides? If so, what was it was like?
3. Make a list of what you think Jesus' hopes, dreams and expectations are for you?
4. What are some of the signs of old age that you have experienced? In what ways can they bring you closer to Jesus? In what ways do they make you question him?

---

[47] John 12:21

"Every man has become brutish and without knowledge; every goldsmith is disappointed by his engraved image; for his molten image is falsehood, and there is no breath in them. They are vanity, a work of delusion: in the time of their visitation they shall perish." - Jeremiah 10:14-15

REMOLDING THE IMAGE

When I was a student in college, I was asked to sign a document stating that I would not plagiarize in my class papers. Being a wise guy, I told my instructor it was impossible for me to sign it. Naturally, he wanted to know why, and I told him it was simple. Everything about me was plagiarized. All I had ever learned had come from someone else. My earliest knowledge came at my mother's knee and in my father's workshop. Later, every bit of me came from teachers, schoolbooks, television shows, radio programs, magazine articles, newspaper reports, movies, and assorted trivial knowledge gained from others. Even the jokes I told were not original. I figured that after it was all boiled down, I was comprised of about ninety-nine point nine percent of world's thinking and a sliver of my own original thought. We both laughed at the idea that I was a totally plagiarized man. And then, he looked over the top of his reading glasses sternly, and I signed the document.

I started thinking. If there really existed a tiny percentage of me that was completely original, how could I find it? Where was this snippet of individuality that was unadulterated, and how could I find him? I knew that throughout history sincere people had tried to find this inner person resulting in countless religions, philosophies, and spiritual ways.

Then I read the words of Jesus who said, "I am the way."

Was it that simple? Was Jesus the way to discover who I was at my innermost core? Could he rescue me from the purloined personality I had become? At first, I did not know what to think. The prospect was too astonishing.

I found a Bible and meditated in the way of the ancients.[48] I studied the enormity of the proposal. At this juncture, I want to point out that meditation and prayer are not the same. Prayer is a request *of* God, and meditation is a reflection *upon* God. As the Psalmist illustrates, "My eyes stay open through the night watches, that I might meditate on your word."[49]

I asked Jesus to show me his way.

Slowly a picture formed of what, or who, was living at the center of my being. Astonishingly, I discovered that at my core I was not alone, and a voice I could not escape came from somewhere deeper asking, "Do you want to be made well?"[50] I responded gladly, "Yes, Lord."

I thought the hard part was over. I assumed that wellness would come in a snap of his fingers, sort of like a playful lark, or a marvelous mystery tour. But, it did not. It began with an embarrassing exposure of the ninety-nine-point-nine percent surrounding my core; a lost man bound hand and foot in the

---

[48] Psalm 5:1

[49] Psalm 119:148

[50] John 5:6

burial rags of the world's sin, arrogance, and ignorance.

Eventually, I came to dimly see the one called the "last Adam" standing at the heart of my heart. He beckoned me closer saying, "I am the Alpha and the Omega, who is and who was and who is to come, the Almighty.[51] If anyone desires to come after me, let him deny himself, take up his cross, and follow me. For whoever desires to save his life will lose it, but whoever will lose his life for my sake, the same will save it."[52]

I tried to come after him, but I was as in a daze, and a maze of worldly thinking. I kept tripping over my plagiarized lusts and illusions.[53] But with each passing day, he patiently revealed another portion of the unplagiarized man as he had always envisioned me. He revealed that he intend me to be something pure. A gender without sexuality, a human without carnality, a person completely unique in character, a soul utterly flawless in composition, and a man unlimited in a sacred capacity known only to him. In short, I was a miraculous cohabitation of spirit and flesh, a blank slate being transformed, and a being fashioned for something greater by his divine power.

But I also learned that the sanctification necessary to cleanse me from my plagiarized life would not be done quickly in a bubble bath of group hugs using the mild soap of tender feelings. My purification would come in a crucible of suffering, just as the prophet Isaiah had foretold, "After the suffering of his soul, he

---

[51] Revelations 1:8

[52] Luke 9:23-24

[53] John 11:44

will see the light and be satisfied."[54]

But I was a soldier once when I was young, and I understood the need and value of suffering. Yet as anyone who has ever served in the military will tell you, it's a soldier's right to complain. And this I did.

Q's

1. List various aspects of your character that have been borrowed from the world. List aspects about your personality that are original to you alone.
2. How can you find the pure one-percent non-plagiarized person as Jesus intends you? What would you expect to find?
3. What is the difference between meditation and prayer? How does each draw us closer to experiencing Jesus who lives at the center of our one percent?

---

[54] Isaiah 53:11

"Most certainly, I tell you, the hour comes, and now is, when the dead will hear the Son of God's voice; and those who hear will live." - John 5:25

HEARING GOD'S VOICE

Most Christians have never heard God's voice. They are troubled by people who say they have. Sometimes they will ask what it sounds like? Or, can they tell if it's from God, or the devil? Some Christians say that only mentally ill people hear voices. Oddly the scriptures are filled with lots of people who heard the voice of God. Why not us? Let's examine how God speaks to people so that we too may hear.

The idea that a person can hear God's voice is usually too weird for the average person to take seriously, much less pursue. Psychiatrists call hearing a voice inside our head an auditory hallucination. So people don't seek the voice of God. They rely on ministers and priests to provide them with lessons on good living, to give them biblical history lessons, tell them what the Scriptures mean, and dictate Christian social norms. In the absence of hearing God's voice for themselves, they settle into a comfortable moral rhythm that moves to the cadence of external religious expectations and internal guilts. Until the day comes in old age when suddenly it doesn't.

Now let's examine where this voice comes from, and why it speaks to us.

When we say that Jesus lives in us we don't mean that there is a physical man running around somewhere inside us. More properly, we mean it is the Holy Spirit who lives in us. "In that day you will know that I am in my Father, and you in me, and I in you."[55]

Think of a lava lamp with two fluid elements encased in a clear container, one floating in the middle of the other. Our human spirit is something like the outer liquid of water, and the Holy Spirit is like an inner liquid of oil moving within our center — quietly and seamlessly. While both are liquids, they are not the same kind. Someday the two must eventually separate because they are incompatible. In the case of God and us, we must eventually separate because his spirit is perfect, and ours is not.

While God has determined that our spirits can coexist for a time on this earth, he has warned us that they cannot coexist forever unless a divine homogenization takes place to create a new spirit emulsion of the two. The agent who serves to create this emulsion of our spirit with God's is Jesus Christ. Without him, God's perfect Spirit, and our imperfect spirit will eventually separate forever. Without Jesus, our imperfect spirit will go to a place that God has created for all imperfection to live. Sometimes this is called hell. Sometimes it is called eternal separation from God.

Our one single job in life is to realize this eventuality, and ask Jesus to act as our sacred homogenizer by transforming our spirit, and blending it with his to save us from eternal separation from God.

---

[55] John 14:20

If this illustration seems muddled, then let's go way, way back to the beginning.

"Come, and you will see."

First, let's ask why would Jesus want the Holy Spirit to live in us?

Imagine that thousands of years ago, there was a planet where the sun had turned into darkness and its moon was the color of blood. The day was night and night was smothered under a thick blanket of gray fog. People born on this planet spent their lives groping around at noonday like blind persons fumbling in the darkness. When they met on the streets in the morning, it was darkness, and when they gathered at noonday it was always the night.[56] This is all the people had ever known, except for the occasional rumors that someday, someone would be born who would bring something by which to see.

For millenniums the people stumbled around bumping into each other, fighting, hating, and suffering the sharp cuts from objects they could not see. Then, on the darkest day in the deepest gloom of night, a single spark of light was struck. And instantly, to all the people sitting in the darkness, it seemed like an enormous glow. Even those who lived far beyond the city in the vast outer regions and the deep valleys covered by the shadow of death, saw that a light had dawned.[57]

They were drawn to the light in curiosity, hoping to touch and be touched by it. When they came near, they were amazed at the source. For there, cradled carefully in a woman's arms, was a baby.

---

[56] Job 5:14

[57] Matt 4:16

From this precious child, light penetrated their soul. People in distant parts of the world sensed that something bright and good had happened, and their hearts longed to know where it was coming from. They were told to seek the child. They journeyed to touch him, and his light leapt out like an electric arc to enter their hearts. They were transformed by a power unknown, but his voice spoke from the light and they were no longer alone, afraid, groping in uncertainty. They wanted to bow down and worship. They wanted to make him happy. They told everyone they met what he had done for them. Soon, the planet was filled with people who had experienced a new way of living. No longer did they fear the darkness and the unknown as a unique voice began guiding them forward.

That's a rough picture of what God is doing by living in us. Jesus chooses to bring the light of his presence into the darkness of our heart to transform us, and the world through us. In the words of Saint Peter, "You are a chosen race, a royal priesthood, a holy nation, a people for God's own possession, that you may proclaim the excellence of him who called you out of darkness into his marvelous light."[58]

If you want Jesus to speak to you, ask him where he lives. Then go there. Be prepared to arise and walk[59] the difficult path he has chosen for you from before you were born. Stay loyal if his voice asks you to follow him into the courtyard of public ridicule. Be steadfast if his voice says you must journey through the garden of

---

[58] 1 Peter 2:9

[59] Luke 5:23

suffering.[60] Be obedient if his voice warns you to resist temptation.[61] Be loyal if his voice asks you to bear tribulations. Stay faithful when you discover that the oil of his light is burned in sacrifice.

Or, you may remain comfortable and secure in your church listening to your minister tell you wonderful stories of easy living, and heavenly delights.

Q's

1. Have you ever heard the voice of Jesus? If so, how did he speak to you? How did you know that it was Jesus?
2. Do you believe that anyone can hear the voice of Jesus if they ask? If not, why not?
3. If Jesus is trying to speak to us, why doesn't he make it easier to hear him? Is it something we are not doing?
4. Write down four things you think he is trying to say to you.

---

[60] Luke 22:44

[61] Luke 22:40

"In this love has been made perfect among us, that we may have boldness in the Day of Judgment, because as he is, even so are we in this world." - 1 John 4:17

ONGOING TRANSFORMATION

As God continues to spark his light in human souls, the power of his voice speaks through billions of human toils and travails, each Christian's life a witness to his truth. From every Christian's lips the story of his redemption is told again and again. They tell the tale of God's joy in blending his spirit with ours to create a new duet singing of glorious tomorrows. Our life is his life, and his life is ours.

In a very real sense God is aging with us. This is a hard lesson, for who can picture a God pouring himself inside our spirit, so that he can share every minute of our life? Who can imagine a God that does not want to possess us, but wants to express us, as we grow older?

Jesus Christ beckons our spirit to join his in a personal journey filled with unexpected challenges, enlightenment, and struggles designed to prepare us for our role in his coming Kingdom, and to cement our faith that we have been chosen for salvation on Judgment Day.

What about Judgment day? For that matter, what about *our* judgment day?

For most of us, it's easier to picture a disembodied spirit being resurrected, than a human body that's been rotting in the grave.

We wonder how the bodies of those lost at sea, or in a fire can be resurrected? And what about our own decaying shell that will soon be laid to rest?

Saint Paul provides us a simple answer. "But if the Spirit of him who raised up Jesus from the dead dwells in you, he who raised up Christ Jesus from the dead will also give life to your mortal bodies through his Spirit who dwells in you."[62]

The good news is that no matter who, what, when, where, why, or how we die, our body will be raised up to live again because it is incorporated into the resurrected body of Jesus by God the Father. And, because the resurrected body of Jesus can never die, our body can never die. We are perpetually connected.

We see the prototype of our new body when Jesus appears to the disciples in Jerusalem after his resurrection and says, "Why are you troubled? Why do doubts arise in your hearts? See my hands and my feet, that it is truly me. Touch me and see, for a spirit doesn't have flesh and bones, as you see that I have."[63]

Again, down at the lake, he shows that his body is still functioning both inside and out when he asks, "'Do you have anything here to eat?' And they gave him a piece of a broiled fish and some honeycomb. He took them, and ate in front of them."[64] Once again, back in the city, Jesus reappeared and showed more physical evidence. Only this time he made a more significant point by saying to Saint Thomas, "Reach here your finger, and see my hands. Reach here your hand, and put it into my side.

---

[62] Romans 8:11

[63] Luke 24:39

[64] Luke 24:41-43

Don't be unbelieving, but believing."[65]

The big lesson is that because Thomas was able to place his finger into the nail holes, and his hand into the spear gash we know that Jesus wounds were not healed, and I believe will not be fully healed until Judgment day when all bodies (including his) will be made right. In his candid display of his unhealed wounds I believe that Jesus wants us to see that even in his resurrected state, he is still very much a human being suffering right along with us. For you and I, that means his suffering includes the pains we experience in aging.

Naturally, the statement that Jesus ages with us is a figure of speech. It is meant to express that Jesus simultaneously experiences our aging through his Holy Spirit, because he has elected to take upon himself our full humanity. He comprehends our physical and spiritual suffering; he feels our daily pains and emotional turmoil caused by our aging mind and decaying body. Because he shares our suffering in real time, he understands us when we get up in the morning upset or depressed. He forgives our frustrations and fickleness.

You can know for yourself if what I say is true. All you have to do is to accept Jesus' challenge to, "'Reach here your hand, and put it into my side. Don't be unbelieving, but believing.'"[66]

---

[65] John 20:27
[66] John 20:27

Q's

1. How do you picture Jesus and the Holy Spirit living within you?
2. Is it rational to believe that Jesus suffers with us, in us? Are we meant to suffer alone while he looks on?
3. In what ways does God age with us? Why would he want to?
4. If Jesus lives in us, can we ever enjoy a moment of pleasure?

"Then the governor's soldiers took Jesus into the Praetorium, and gathered the whole garrison together against him. They stripped him, and put a scarlet robe on him. They braided a crown of thorns and put it on his head, and a reed in his right hand; and they kneeled down before him, and mocked him, saying, 'Hail, King of the Jews!' They spat on him, and took the reed and struck him on the head." - Matthew 27:27-30

SINNERS IN THE HANDS

What about our sins? Can a perfect Jesus live in an imperfect sinner? Does he experience our sins? The short answer is yes. He experiences every one of our sins as a betraying slap across his face, a disappointing glob of spittle in his eye, another sorrowful thorn in his crown, and a depressing lash across his back. Yes, Jesus still suffers. However, Jesus does not sin with us; he patiently takes our sins from us to effect our sanctification, and ultimate salvation.

Ministers who earn a living condemning sinners in a never-ending litany of moral outrage make having a relationship with Jesus virtually impossible. In the case of old people, it's hard enough to feel good about our situation much less be attracted to an angry God in constant need of our apologetic affirmation. Ministers of the aggrieved God who is never satisfied with our human foibles not only question the salvation of their flock, but they condemn us to a hellish cycle of contrived guilt, and forced repentance. Only a spiritual masochist needs to attend a weekly drubbing of religious blame and shame. The rest of us will stay away from the cruel pulpits of the self-righteousness.

On the other hand, ministers who preach an indulgent God, make having a relationship with Jesus virtually unnecessary. In a church where God is preoccupied with dismissing our sins so that we can feel good about ourselves, there is no call for the sober posture of spiritual responsibility beyond that of diplomatic sensitivity. Ministers of the open-minded God not only make a mockery of the depravity of the human heart as depicted in the Bible, but they deceive their listeners in a weekly message of self-importance. We will flee the pulpits of biblical fluidity where God exists only as a moral guide, and where virtue is practiced in the abstract.

In my opinion, God can be more rightly viewed as a loving pragmatist who sees the deathly impact that our sins have upon our relationship with him, others, and ourselves. In this view he doesn't see us as bad people who need to be constantly rebuked, admonished and punished; nor is he permissive or dismissive concerning our sins. Instead, he sees us as fallen people whose sins are forgiven through our willing obedience to his desires. When he tells us, "You are my friends, if you do whatever I command you,"[67] he sets the standard for a forgiving relationship. When Jesus says, "Go and sin no more," he is not expecting our perfection, he is expecting that we will do our utmost.

[67] John 15:14

Q's

1. How have your sins changed over the years? What sins do you struggle with, as you have grown older?
2. Do you feel forgiven by God? If so, what makes you feel this? If not, why not?
3. There are sins of commission, and sins of omission. Make a mental list of each kind that you are guilty of?
4. What does Jesus command of his friends?

PART THREE

GROWING SUFFERING

"He was despised, and rejected by men; a man of suffering, and acquainted with disease. He was despised as one from whom men hide their face; and we didn't respect him. Surely he has borne our sickness, and carried our suffering; yet we considered him plagued, struck by God, and afflicted." - Isaiah 53:3-6

THE WAY OF THE WAY

If Jesus is the Way, then what is the way of Jesus? Some say his way is found in social justice, heartfelt compassion, racial equality, women's rights, gender diversity, political reform, sexual inclusion, love, and peace. Rarely will you hear anyone say that his way is found in sacrifice, suffering, and sorrow. Yet that is exactly what Jesus modeled over the course of his life; especially in the last twenty-four hours.

Starting with the depressing betrayal by Judas, and ending with his agonizing moment-by-moment death on the cross, he showed us the road we must travel in life, especially at its end.[68] Saint John of the Cross made this point abundantly clear. "The road is narrow. He who wishes to travel it more easily must cast off all things and use the cross as his cane. He must be truly resolved to suffer willingly for the love of God in all things."[69]

No one denies that our lives are filled with suffering in some form or another. The unborn, little babies, children, youth, and

[68] The last 24 hours of Jesus' life is recorded in Matthew 26:14-27:66; Mark 14:10-15:47; Luke 22:1-23:56; and John 11:55-19:42.

[69] Dark Night of the Soul, Dover Thrift Editions, Paperback, May 9, 2003

middle-aged all have their special growing pains and miseries. Yet for those of us who will grow old, there is particular suffering waiting for us. And it will come without our asking.

You may remember back in the 1960s when the United States Government drafted men into military service to fight in Viet Nam. Many unhappy souls ran to Canada or joined the seminary to avoid the draft. Men with no other options went kicking, cussing, and screaming to basic training where they were given their first taste of real suffering. Yet, despite their original misgivings, most served their country honorably. Fifty years later, I see these guys proudly wearing their "Viet Nam Veteran" ball caps. Every one of them I encounter has told me that they consider themselves better men for having suffered for a greater cause in the jungles of South East Asia.

In some ways old age is like God's draft, except no one can dodge it. It's a special theater of spiritual warfare that provides an opportunity for greater service to God in the final years of our lives. If we are willing to see it for what it is, old age can be a time of extraordinary usefulness that someday we will take exceeding joy in. Perhaps we will see men and women in heaven wearing their "Suffering Saint" ball cap, and they will be grateful that God drafted them for a greater cause.

Are you ready to earn your cap? If so, take heart in the scripture that says, "Because you are partakers of Christ's sufferings, rejoice; that at the revelation of his glory you also may rejoice with exceeding joy."[70]

---

[70] 1 Peter 4:13

Q's

1. In what ways do you mentally and/or physically suffer? How does your suffering impact your spirit?
2. Do you think a Christian should have to suffer in order to follow the Way?
3. Does suffering make people better or stronger? If so, how?
4. In what ways can the suffering of an older person be useful to God?

ME SUFFER?

At this juncture, it is not my intention to provide a theology of suffering. I will only say that suffering is a fact of life, a major theme in the Bible and the central act in the life of Jesus. The modern Protestant church largely ignores it, and the elderly have suffered spiritually because of it.

So, let's take a closer look.

Let's assume that suffering didn't just fall out of the sky, but originated in some way. The Bible says the cause of suffering traces back to our original parents Adam and Eve. As the story goes, they broke their perfect non-suffering communion with God through their willful disobedience of him. The result was as follows: "To the woman God said, "I will greatly multiply your pain in childbirth. In pain you will bear children. To Adam he said, "Because you have listened to your wife's voice, and have eaten of the tree, of which I commanded you, saying, 'You shall not eat of it,' cursed is the ground for your sake. In toil you will eat of it all the days of your life."[71]

In other words, pain and toil would equate to suffering and sweat.

Other religions have their own explanations about the origin of suffering. Oddly, Christianity is the only religion that says we are to rejoice in our sufferings. As Saint Paul says, "We also rejoice in our sufferings, knowing that suffering works perseverance; and

---

[71] Geneses 16:17

perseverance, proven character; and proven character, hope."[72]

Let's say that suffering can be broken into two types. The first is that which is deserved, and the second is that which is innocent. Deserved suffering is a consequence of our own actions. For example, when a robber is caught stealing, she is put in jail and suffers. When a man decides to climb a mountain and breaks a leg, he suffers. People who suffer due to their own actions normally accept their pain as the legitimate result of their decisions. Even the suffering thief on the cross was objective enough to take responsibility for his actions. "For we receive the due reward for our deeds, but this man has done nothing wrong."[73]

On the other hand, innocent suffering is not a consequence of our actions. It is the result of other people or forces we have no control over, such as hurricanes, epidemics, evildoers, and old age. Yet despite what the Bible says about how we are to rejoice in our sufferings, I've never met a Christian who prayed for cancer as a way to generate a proven character. I've never spoken to a survivor of a natural disaster who told me that they rejoiced in their suffering when their home and/or family were wiped out. Most people want relief from their suffering, not religious platitudes. They want an explanation, not evangelization. They just want the pain to stop.

---

[72] Romans 5:3

[73] Luke 23:41

Q's

1. Why do you think there is suffering in the world?
2. Do you believe that God is unfair? If so, why? If not, why not?
3. Have you ever experienced deserved suffering? What did you do? Have you ever experienced innocent suffering? How did you react?
4. What kind of innocent suffering is experienced in old age? What kind of deserved suffering takes place?

THE SUFFERING MAN

The concept of suffering is woven throughout the Bible. There are two principle characters that demonstrate how we should deal with it. In the Old Testament, there is Job (pronounced Joab), "For there is none like him in the earth, a blameless and an upright man, one who fears God, and turns away from evil."[74] And in the New Testament, there is Jesus who is the Word made flesh[75] and Prince of Peace.[76]

Considered the oldest book in the Bible, the story of Job highlights how important our spiritual forefathers viewed the problem of suffering. It examines Job's response to innocent suffering, and whether it is appropriate to ever blame God for our suffering. We learn that we are not the first to ask God questions about our afflictions. For example, Job wonders how anyone can ever appease an invisible God who cannot be swayed by human persuasion? He asks why God judges people if he has the power to simply forgive, or change their actions? Six centuries before the birth of Jesus, Job was even able to reason that there must exist a "witness" in heaven to help him in his suffering, "Even now, behold, my witness is in heaven. He who vouches for me is on high."[77]

As a consequence of his suffering Job arrives at one of the most

---

[74] Job 1:8
[75] John 1:14
[76] Isaiah 9:6
[77] Job 16:19

important statements of faith in the Old Testament, "But as for me, I know that my Redeemer lives. In the end, he will stand upon the earth. After my skin is destroyed, then in my flesh shall I see God, Whom I shall see on my side? My eyes shall see, and not as a stranger."[78]

Here are some of the key lessons of faith we learn from the chronicle of Job's suffering.

- Satan exists.
- Sin did not cause Job's suffering.
- God allows suffering for a purpose known only to him.
- Justice is not dispensed using a variable scale.
- Job is not a patient man; he is a persevering man.
- God doesn't punish us for asking questions when we suffer.
- Suffering is proportionate to each individual.
- Suffering is limited in scope by God.
- Don't ask why many good people suffer, and why many bad ones don't.
- God may not answer our prayers, but he's not deaf. He hears our cries.
- We shouldn't demand that God justify himself to us.
- Not everything in life is equitable, but God is not unfair.
- Divine justice is taking place; we don't know how God is implementing it.

---

[78] Job 19: 25

- Family and friends mean well, but they can disappoint us when we suffer.
- God richly blessed Job for his faith during his suffering.

When we compare the suffering accounts of Job and Jesus, we see five key differences between these two men:

1. Job *questions* why we suffer, and Jesus *answers* why we suffer.
2. Job gives us insight into suffering by watching the reactions of a *mortal* man, and Jesus gives us insight into suffering by watching the reactions of a *divine* man.
3. Job suffers *fatalistically*, and Jesus suffers *faithfully*.
4. Job *resists* his suffering, and Jesus *accepts* his suffering.
5. Job is the *victim* of suffering, and Jesus is the *victor* of suffering.

When taken together, the two accounts provide a complete understanding of why, and how we are to suffer.

Q's

1. Have you ever felt that God struck you, or someone you love with unexplainable innocent suffering? How did you feel about that?
2. What are some appropriate ways for a Christian to react to unexplainable innocent suffering?
3. Is it ever okay to be angry with God?

THE SUFFERING WOMAN

The spiritual sufferings of a woman need special attention. The story of Job may provide us with broad explanations about human suffering, but what of those sufferings unique to a woman? We find those answers in the story of a person that Protestants generally ignore except at Christmastime when we hear the name of Mary. Yet this person is arguably the second most important person in the scriptures.

I do not deify Mary; she is not God, just the closest person to God. I respect that she holds the key to many of the mysteries about the nature of Jesus. After all, she is his mother. Her spirit is filled with grace, and her heart holds the depth of Jesus' human personality.

She bore his suffering as only a mother can. "Simeon blessed them, and said to Mary, his mother, "Behold, this child is set for the falling and the rising of many in Israel, and for a sign which is spoken against. Yes, a sword will pierce through your own soul, that the thoughts of many hearts may be revealed."[79] There is a good reason why Mary became known to the early church as the Mother of Sorrows.

Why do so many people feel a kinship to Mary? Because many of them believe that when Christians die they immediately live again as a member of the community of saints in heaven while waiting for God's final judgment. They also believe that the Holy

---

[79] Luke 2:34

Spirit living in all Christians connects those alive on earth with those alive in heaven. Therefore, if the Holy Spirit lives in Mary, she is connected to Christ and us.

But there is a difference. She holds a special relationship with him that we can never have. It began when the angel Gabriel told her, "The Holy Spirit will come on you, and the power of the Most High will overshadow you. Therefore the holy one who is born from you will be called the Son of God."[80]

Of course there is also the mundane fact that she carried him for nine months, bore him in suffering and pain, nursed him from her breast, wiped his bottom, taught him to walk, nurtured the first words out of his mouth, protected him from the sword of Herod, made him snacks as a child, helped him through puberty, followed him in his ministry, watched him experience a hideous death, placed him in his tomb, and was in one accord with all of the disciples in the upper room in Jerusalem. For these and other reasons, this remarkable woman deserves our attention.

There are thousands of books you can read about Mary so I don't intend to stray into the world of Mariology. But it's important to consider the special place that his mother held in Jesus' heart, and why by studying her suffering, a Christian woman can learn much about how to deal with their own suffering as they age.

There is nothing magical about Mary. If anything she is presented as a down to earth woman who is modest, pure, direct, unflappable and doggedly faithful to her calling, her family and

[80] Luke 1:35

Yahweh. In the person of Mary, we are given a unique window into the heart of a woman afflicted at many levels with physical, emotional and spiritual pain. From her backbreaking eighty mile journey on a donkey to Bethlehem during her last trimester, her shedding of blood bringing Jesus into the world, her flight into Egypt to escape Herod's assassins, her heart stopping worry after losing the child Jesus in the Temple, her grief over the death of her husband Joseph, her misery as Jesus was flayed and crucified, and her faithful resolve as a widow living into old age, Mary suffered as only a woman can. Moreover, she participated with Jesus in his divine suffering step by step throughout his entire life, culminating at the foot of the cross.

Most Protestants have been raised to view Mary as part of the supporting cast in a Christmas pageant where her role is to be the tender young mother kneeling at the manager. But if we take a closer look at this person, we find a no-nonsense girl who bravely accepts the call of God to venture into a supernatural reality that the world had never known. From the time of Jesus' birth Mary knew that her life would never be one of domestic tranquility. She realized early that her sacred destiny would mean that she would help Jesus grow to manhood, release him into the world, and be at his side when the executioners came. Why? Because she understood what Simeon meant when he told her, "this child is set for the falling and the rising of many in Israel."[81]

This is why we offend Jesus when we dismiss Mary as a stage prop or underestimate his feelings for her. I wince when I hear

---

[81] Luke 2:34

Christians insult her with ignorant slurs of being nothing more than a manifestation of some Egyptian goddess like Isis. If Jesus is like any normal man who hears someone insult his mother, he will take it personally. I realize it's hard for us to picture Jesus having normal human feelings for his mother. We have not been taught to think that he has a special attachment to her. But he does. He loves her as much as I love my own mother, and my son loves his. So it's not being superstitious to want to avoid raising the ire of my master by offending his mother. Instead I believe that he appreciates our respect when we take notice of her many wonderful qualities, all of which point us to her divine son.

One look at the following humorous exchange between the two, and we see an excellent example of their close bond. In this story Jesus is presented as a good Jewish son who is a sociable guy and obedient to his mother. We are at a wedding feast in the town of Cana where he performs his first recorded miracle against his better wishes. "The third day, there was a marriage in Cana of Galilee. Jesus' mother was there. Jesus also was invited, with his disciples, to the marriage. When the wine ran out, Jesus' mother said to him, "They have no wine." Jesus said to her, "Woman, what does that have to do with you and me? My hour has not yet come." His mother said to the servants, "Whatever he says to you, do it."[82]

Can you picture the look on Mary's face when Jesus said, "My hour has not yet come." Yeah, right. Try saying that to your mother when she "suggests" that you do something. As you can

---

[82] John 2:1-4

imagine, the very next minute Jesus was ordering the servants to, "Fill the water pots with water."[83] And you know the rest of the story.

Mary doesn't have some form of supernatural control over Jesus any more than my mother has mystical powers over me. It's just that they have a special mother and son connection unlike any other in creation. Think about the final thoughts of Jesus while he suffered on the cross as he uttered the first words of Psalm 22, "My God, my God. Why have you forsaken me?" Many people don't realize that the Psalm goes on to say, "You brought me out of the womb. You made me trust at my mother's breasts. I was thrown on you from my mother's womb. You are my God since my mother bore me. Don't be far from me, for trouble is near. For there is none to help."[84]

Protestants who fear Mary have no reason to. Mary has as much to say to us about Jesus as Saint Paul does, who has taken on a cult like status within the Protestant circles. However, in Mary's case we do not learn about our relationship to Jesus from reading her words, as much as we do by observing her actions.

And we shouldn't blame Mary for the enthusiasm of an ancient church that fashioned doctrines and teachings about her that arguably fall outside of biblical revelation. Yet just by staying within the pages of the Bible we can find a treasure trove of enlightenment that is undoubtedly more important than listening to a sermon on Esther, Ruth, or Hannah.

The problem with Mary, like so many people in the Bible, is

---

[83] John 2:7
[84] Psalm 22: 9

that we must use our Christian imagination to fill in some of the blanks of her story. We must call upon the Holy Spirit to open our eyes to the girl behind the woman who became the mother of Jesus. Our study of this woman does not suddenly elevate her beyond her own stated desire to be the humble servant of God, "Behold, the handmaid of the Lord; be it to me according to your word."[85] It simply helps us to unlock the richness of the scriptures found in the story of this singularly unique woman.

When we take Mary seriously, we can ask the Holy Spirit a wider range of questions related to our own life and suffering. If you are a woman you can ask the Holy Spirit questions like, "How did Mary handle the suffering of riding a donkey for eighty miles during her third trimester?" "What worries did she have about her husband and son?" "What are some of the things about godly character she would have taught Jesus as a child?" "Why did she insist he do something at the wedding feast in Cana?" "What did Simeon mean when he said her heart would be pierced?" "How did she keep from losing her mind with grief at the death of Jesus?" "How did she deal with the terror of being hunted down by Herod's assassins?" "How did she manage as a single mother after the loss of her husband Joseph?" "Why didn't she quarrel with Jesus when he placed her in the care of John?" "Why was belonging to the community in Jerusalem important to Mary after Jesus ascended?" "In what ways did the community support Mary after Jesus was gone?" "What did Mary give to the community?"

[85] Luke 1:38

I am sure that you can come up with many more questions of your own.

Pondering these and other questions does not discredit or threaten her son. He gave her to us along with every other character in the scriptures so that their lives could be examined and discussed to add light to our understanding of him. What better life to study than the one closest to his?

As we age, it's important that we consider the unique suffering of Mary, especially if you are a woman. When we get to heaven, we will all have to pay her special gratitude and thank her for helping to shape the boy who grew into a man who was born to suffer, sacrifice and save us from our sins, and ourselves.

Q's

1. Do you think that reading about Mary in the Bible can provide you with helpful insights into your own life? If so, in what ways?
2. How do women handle suffering differently from men?

WHY SUFFER?

Of course the short answer to the question of why we suffer is — why not? Do we really expect that we are untouchable in a world of cold brutality and cruel hearts? Do we really imagine escaping mental issues, deformed bodies or capricious disease? The beautiful people think they can. But when old age comes, even they find suffering is waiting for them. The harsh fact is that nobody escapes suffering. The psalmist wrote, "I am weary with my groaning. Every night I flood my bed. I drench my couch with my tears."[86]

Jesus, in the Gospel of John provides the long answer to the question of why we suffer. "As he passed by, he saw a man blind from birth. His disciples asked him, "Rabbi, who sinned, this man or his parents, that he was born blind?" Jesus answered, "Neither did this man sin, nor his parents; but, that the works of God might be revealed in him."[87] The good news found in this story is that we learn that God allows a Christian to suffer in this world so that his works might be revealed in them.

Are you suffering right now? Would you like to believe that you have been chosen by God to have his works revealed through you? Wouldn't you like to think that your suffering isn't some freakish accident, but is being permitted for a reason? If we can look upon our suffering in that light, it might not make our

---

[86] Psalm 6:6

[87] John 9:1

suffering any easier but it gives it a divine meaning that we can understand and live with.

When dealing with the question of our suffering, the answer will not come in a few neatly quoted scriptures, or inspirational words from a minister. It will not be found in a solution provided by a doctor, or a pill from a pharmaceutical company. Addressing our suffering will require a different approach because the kind of suffering that comes with old age falls in its own category, it is one of the most vile of all torments.

Unfortunately no one but another senior can understand the horrifying ways it impacts our life. It is neither inflicted upon us by others, nor is it a self-inflicted punishment. For the first time in our lives we are the helpless victims of aging bodies and deteriorating minds that we have lost control of. We are frail targets to be bullied, robbed, shamed, and mocked. We are the victims of systems that squeeze every penny out of our social security, savings and pensions. We are the shut-ins, forgotten by busy relatives. We are the abandoned, isolated by society. We are the old, facing a future filled with doom, paranoia and fear. The rich cannot bribe their way out, and the poor cannot run away. We are too proud to cry out, too stubborn to seek help, and too humiliated to ask for special attention. We are trapped in a special kind of misery from which there is no earthly escape.

Q's

1. In what ways are you suffering now?
2. Do you think that any good can come from your suffering?
3. Have you ever known a Christian who became embittered in the last years of their lives? What caused it?
4. How will you keep from becoming soured by suffering?

INESCAPABLE SUFFERING

So who wants to suffer? I'm willing to if I can keep suffering on an academic level. It's easy enough to write about it, but in the cold hard light of a minor stroke or blinding depression, not so much. Yet suffering is inescapable. It's how we face it that matters.

There are at least three ways to approach it. The first is to accept its inevitability. The second is to prepare for it. The third is to find comfort in the knowledge that God has selected us for a "higher education" of the soul. As Saint Ignatius Loyola said, "If God sends you many sufferings, it is a sign that He has great plans for you."[88]

When we recognize that there is a greater plan intended in our suffering then we can seek its meaning. If we can find its meaning then we can define its purpose, and if we can find it's purpose then our suffering can become a tool to manifest God's grace and truth.

Waiting until we are forced to suffer to find the grace of Jesus is ridiculous. There is no need to wait. We suffer every day in large and small ways. Some of us suffer crippling depression, anxiety and insecurities that make it difficult to get out of bed in the morning. Others suffer physical ailments that bring them a variety of pain all day. Millions suffer from hunger, mistreatment and armed conflicts. Most of us just suffer the normal aches, pains, and worries of life.

---

[88] Saint Ignatius Loyola

Typical of his character, God takes the bad and turns it into good. In the case of suffering he uses it draw us closer. Suffering often results in the intensity of concentration necessary to intersect our human life with God's divine love. Take the case of the prodigal son who decided to reunite with his father because of his suffering. Or the story of the suffering thief on the cross who found God hanging right next to him. In both cases, the purpose of suffering was to bring reconciliation with God. In the case of the wayward son, it was through a long process. With the thief on the cross, it was in a very brief period.

Which brings us to the greatest calling of our life: to participate in Jesus' ongoing work of saving love by uniting our sacrifice and suffering with his. "Therefore I urge you, by the mercies of God, to present your bodies a living sacrifice, holy, acceptable to God, which is your spiritual service."[89]

Regrettably most churches don't teach people how or why they must suffer. When preachers say, "Jesus died for your sins" they omit half the gospel. Jesus did more than just die for our sins. He came down from heaven and suffered a lifetime of living in an undeveloped land without the comforts of modern medicine or technology. He existed under the oppressive hand of brutal soldiers who occupied his country. He experienced satanic torment, personal heartbreak and physical discomfort. And then, in the final twenty-four hours of his life, he suffered every emotional and physical pain imaginable.

Why?

---

[89] Romans 12:1

So that we might see for ourselves that the fullness of God's love is perfected and made visible through suffering. When the Lord spoke to Ananias about Saint Paul he said, "For he is my chosen vessel to bear my name before the nations and kings, and the children of Israel. For I will show how many things he must suffer for my name's sake."[90]

Are you God's chosen vessel to suffer for his name's sake? If you must be dragged through your suffering begrudgingly, haltingly, grumbling like you have been cursed, you will forfeit any opportunity to encounter the divine purpose you have been seeking all your life.

Maybe you're wondering where God's love is found in suffering? Your minister told you that divine love is found in blessings, success, pleasant feelings and peaceful thoughts. They are wrong. You're hearing a theological position designed to keep you happy so that you'll keep coming back to their church. If people were told that Jesus expects them to really, really, actually, honestly suffer with him, they would find a church somewhere else.

Don't think that his suffering was relegated to the streets of Jerusalem two thousand years ago so that we could all go to heaven. His suffering is a current ongoing activity that Jesus experiences right now through his people where he grieves, cries, and endures their pain, and mental anguish.

How do we know this?

Let's revisit the story of his bodily presentation to Saint

---

[90] Acts 9:15

Thomas. "Then he said to Thomas, "Reach here your finger, and see my hands. Reach here your hand, and put it into my side. Don't be unbelieving, but believing."[91] In this short verse we learn that Jesus' wounds were not healed because Thomas could place his finger in the holes. This is an important detail that is normally overlooked in our rush to condemn Thomas as an unworthy skeptic. The bigger picture is that even in his resurrected body Jesus' wounds had not yet mended.

What are we to make of this fact?

It is an indication that they will not heal, and his suffering will not stop until his people's wounds are healed, and their suffering stops which will occur on Judgment Day. Then his wounds will close and he will drink from the cup of final redemption. "But I tell you that I will not drink of this fruit of the vine from now on, until that day when I drink it anew with you in my Father's Kingdom."[92]

Additionally, Saint Paul gives compelling evidence that Jesus continued to suffer after his ascension when he wrote of his own personal desire for fellowship in the suffering of Jesus, "That I may know him, and the power of his resurrection, and the fellowship of his sufferings."[93] We may assume that Paul couldn't know Jesus in the fellowship of his sufferings, if Jesus no longer suffered.

Another important clue is given when Paul uses the words "fellowship *in* the suffering." In New Testament Greek the word

---

[91] John 20:27

[92] Matthew 26:29

[93] Philippians 3:10

for fellowship is koinonia meaning, "joint participation." Authentic joint participation takes place in the *present* moment, not as a symbolic homage to a *past* memory. Which is why Jesus tells us to take the bread and wine in the present memory of him, not as a memory of the past. "Do this *in memory* of me," he says. Not *as memory* of me. True communion with God is a joint participation with him in the present moment that joins his soul to ours.

Some other important ways to have joint participation with God are in receiving his wisdom through meditation, his presence in prayer, his strength in sacrifice, and his grace through suffering. These are all voluntary undertakings on our part. When he says, "If anyone desires to come after me, let him deny himself, and take up his cross, and follow me," it is more of a request than a demand.

Theologically we might say that Jesus accomplished the first half of our salvation in his death at the cross, and the final act of our salvation is taking place right now in his real time suffering with us as we bear our own cross with him. On judgment day when salvation will be complete, one way that Jesus will identify the people who have done the will of his Father will be to observe those who have joined their suffering to his. "Not everyone who says to me, 'Lord, Lord,' shall enter the kingdom of heaven, but he who does the will of My Father in heaven."[94]

What is the will of the Father?

It is for us to humbly accept whatever suffering he permits in

---

[94] Matthew 7:21

our life, and to use it as an evangelical witness of his divine love so that our friends, family and medical practitioners may visibly see what divine love looks like, and be brought to their own redemption.

Many Christians do not believe that Jesus still suffers. They think that Jesus has already suffered for all of us so that we no longer have to. Which is why so many Christians are surprised when they experience suffering in old age. They have no teachings to help them understand or deal with the magnitude of what they are going through. But ask yourself, if Jesus does not suffer with us, then how can we ever hope to find a meaning to our suffering? If he has already suffered for all of us, then how do we explain the suffering we are going through? What is the point of our suffering if there is nothing to be gained from it?

In the final years of our lives we may find that our suffering is real, lonely, seemingly endless and without apparent meaning. If Jesus does not participate in our suffering then we can expect nothing but an echoless silence when we scream to the heavens from the bottom of the pit.

Betsie ten Boom reflected on this possibility as she suffered waiting for execution as a prisoner in the Ravensbruck concentration camp. She confided to her sister Corrie that, "There is no pit so deep that he is not deeper still."[95] Meaning that no matter how deep our suffering is, Jesus suffers more.

The good news is that the same Jesus, who suffered with Betsie and her sister Corrie in the Nazi concentration camp, is with us

---

[95] As related by her sister, and fellow prisoner, Corrie ten Boom.

right now sharing our personal prison of pain, hospital of agony or straitjacket of fear that we are trapped in. We can depend that his voice of comfort will be heard when we reach the bottom of the pit, and our world has gone silent.

Q's

1. How do you think the fullness of God's love is perfected, and made visible through suffering?
2. Must suffering always be endured passively, or is there a way to utilize it?
3. Can you prepare your soul for suffering? If so, what would you do?
4. Is there a way out of the depths of the dark pit? How?

SUFFERING SALVATION

In the traditional Protestant view, Calvary is the place where Jesus died so that we could be saved and go to heaven. While that might be true, it is not the fullness of truth because it places all of the emphasis of our salvation on his death, and none on his suffering. Moreover, it does not explain the rational behind why he suffered. After all, suffering and death are not the same things.

To help understand the difference, think of his suffering and death as two separate parts of a divine formula, sort of like taking two chemical components and mixing them to form an epoxy. In everyday language we would call these two components a hardener and resin. Let's say that the hardener is his suffering, and the resin is his death. When added together they form a supernatural epoxy that bonds us permanently to God. The bond created is supernaturally flawless because Jesus cured it through his perfect emotional, spiritual and fleshly suffering right down to the last drop of his blood. It is through this action that he took our sins into himself, died with them upon the cross, and extinguished them into the abyss. Through his stripes and death he provided us the only bond that can ever cement us to God so that we may live to righteousness, and experience spiritual healing.[96] We call this process our sanctification, and salvation.

His suffering also provides us tangible evidence that there is no

---

[96] 1 Peter 2:24

complimentary grace that just floats down from heaven empty of pain. By dragging his cross up the hill of death under the torturous blows and whips of the centurions, he demonstrated the way we must all endure our life in order to fully participate in his.

When we glibly say that, "Jesus already paid the price for us" without accepting our role in that price, we show a remarkable ignorance of the expenditure required to effect our eternal salvation. If there is no need to participate in his suffering, then what do we make of the biblical requirement to "work out your own salvation with fear and trembling?"[97] How can we "work out" our salvation without suffering? Can we obtain it through good deeds and pleasant thoughts?

Whenever we reject, avoid, deny or dismiss suffering as being inconsistent with the nature of a loving God, we show the world that we don't understand what divine love is. An authentic Christian life in Jesus is a daily expression of our co-partnering with his suffering love. It is the only kind of love that explains Jesus to atheists, demonstrates the gospel to skeptics, and redeems the wretched. Moreover it is the only kind of love that provides the sacred grace to grow our soul.

How can a soul grow you ask?

We know that the phrases "Kingdom of God" and "Kingdom of Heaven" can be used interchangeably. Jesus tells the Pharisees, "The Kingdom of God is within you."[98] Then in the Gospel of Matthew he says, "The Kingdom of Heaven is like a grain of mustard seed, which a man took, and sowed in his field; which

---

[97] Philippians 2:12b
[98] Luke 17:21

indeed is smaller than all seeds. But when it is grown, it is greater than the herbs, and becomes a tree, so that the birds of the air come and lodge in its branches."[99] Presumably God has placed no limits upon the growth of his kingdom within us, which means that as his kingdom grows so does our soul.

Let's say there are two Christians. One has grown their soul to the size of a thimble, and one the size of a massive oil tanker. Let's fill them both to the brim with divine grace. Are they both filled to one hundred percent of their capacity? Yes. Do they both contain the same amount of grace? No. Which of the two souls would you rather have when you enter the gates of heaven, the one the size of a thimble or the one the size of an oil tanker? Which of the two people do you think will have the greatest ability to enjoy the beatific vision, divine love and presence of God forever?

Divine love, found through suffering in old age, is the ordinary saint's chance to grow in grace and expand the kingdom of heaven within them. The opportunity to increase in grace is not limited to weekly communion, worship or prayer time when we are comfortably seated in our pews. It takes place every day in our suffering fibromyalgia or psychological stress. It happens during our depression and dental problems. It occurs in ALS and chemotherapy. It strikes during the collapse of our investments, a flood that wipes away our home or the loss of a job.

During suffering times like these we have a choice. We can hate our life, walk around dazed and confused, curse God, and

[99] Matthew 13:31

continue to die. Or, we can give thanks to God that it wasn't worse, and offer our suffering to him like a drink offering. Suffering with Jesus opens us to an understanding that there is more going on in the Kingdom of God than we think. Suffering humbles us so that we can truly love our neighbor. It prepares us for our coming service to God in heaven,[100] and it is a painful reminder to, "Trust in Yahweh with all your heart, and don't lean on your own understanding."[101]

I recall the story of a pastor who visited a terminally ill member of his congregation. It was late at night and the lights in the hospital room were dim. The man had just undergone a round of chemotherapy. After watching him endure several violent fits of vomiting, the pastor gently reminded the man that because he was terminally ill he didn't have to continue with the chemo treatments. The man weakly replied that he wasn't doing them for himself, but for his wife. The pastor was confused.

"For your wife?"

"Yes pastor," the man said. "I want her to have the comfort of knowing that I've done everything I could to live a little longer."

"But I don't understand why you have to suffer so much," the pastor said.

With that, the man looked up and replied, "I don't know either pastor, but God must be allowing it for my good."[102]

---

[100] Revelation 22:33
[101] Proverbs 3:5
[102] Romans 8:28

Q's

1. Do you think that your soul can grow? Why would it be a good thing? How do you think you would change if it did?
2. What did Paul mean when he wrote, "work out our own salvation with fear and trembling?"
3. In what ways can God use suffering for your good?

SUFFERING HARDSHIP

Suffering is the primary condition of our world. Simply because we accept Jesus Christ as Lord and Savior we are not protected from suffering. Why? Because when we decide to follow Jesus we agree to join in his suffering for the world's salvation. As the martyr Dietrich Bonhoeffer defined it, "A Christian is someone who shares the sufferings of God in the world."

Today's corporate church presents a gospel of benefits without any requirement to sacrifice, or suffer beyond an occasional inconvenience. Nothing is further from the gospel truth. Jesus goes out of his way to remind his followers "Don't be afraid of the things which you are about to suffer. Behold, the devil is about to throw some of you into prison that you may be tested; and you will have oppression for ten days.[103] Be faithful to death, and I will give you the crown of life."[104] One way to interpret his words is to say that we will all be thrown into the prison of old age where we will be tested by suffering for a limited time.

I've heard some Christians speak of "unjust" suffering. There is no such thing. The idea of injustice comes from the mind of Satan who invented the concept, and sold it to Eve when he suggested that God was unjust because he had withheld information from her. "For God knows that in the day you eat it,

---

[103] The number ten in the Bible signifies completeness over the course of time or completeness in divine order.

[104] Revelations 2:10

your eyes will be opened, and you will be like God."[105] Satan still whispers to each of us that God is unjust, and to blame him for allowing all of the suffering in the world, especially our own. But our suffering is not unjust. It is pure cause and effect.

The cause was Adam and Eve believing that God was unfair which generated a feeling of resentment that resulted in their willful disobedience to his command not to eat of the tree. All of this ended with their expulsion from the perfect garden of life into a world of suffering that they created with the help of Satan. "Therefore Yahweh God sent him out from the Garden of Eden, to till the ground from which he was taken."[106]

You and I were born into this world of suffering. Instead of thinking that our suffering is unfair, we should be grateful that we don't suffer even more, and for Jesus saving us from eternal suffering. Until then we must persevere in our sufferings with a deliberate faith that a loving God, for our eternal good, will use our suffering to accomplish his divine plan.

Q's

1. Do you believe that a Christian should suffer?
2. What would be the worst way for you to suffer? How could you find God's goodness in it?
3. Have you ever felt that God was unfair to you, or someone else? If so, how did you deal with that?

---

[105] Genesis 3:5

[106] Genesis 3:23

SUFFERING SPIRIT

The vast majority of modern Protestant churches seem indifferent to suffering in old age. Many believe that suffering is curable by "getting right with God." But spiritual suffering in old age is something all together different. It is not a matter of "getting right with God." It is the result of a damaged mind, broken body or beaten soul, not God's retribution. It is not localized to a specific pain or emotional feeling. It shadows our days, infiltrates our thoughts and incapacitates our desires. "Have mercy on me, Yahweh, for I am faint. Yahweh, heal me, for my bones are troubled. My soul is also in great anguish."[107]

Spiritual suffering is more than depression, greater than nausea and incurable using modern medicine, physical therapy or psychiatry. It is a form of torment that strikes at the very core of a person's soul leading to a supernatural anguish that King David describes as the pit of darkness. Jesus experienced the pit of darkness so deeply in the garden of Gethsemane that his skin broke into a sweat of blood. "Being in agony he prayed more earnestly. His sweat became like great drops of blood falling down on the ground."[108]

In a previous section we learned that through his suffering Jesus showed us the immeasurable depth of God's divine love. It

---

[107] Psalm 6:2

[108] Luke 22:44

is a love willing to come down from heaven into the pit of our spiritual darkness, and suffer the incomparable misery of being a human with us. "He said to them, "See my hands and my feet, that it is truly me. Touch me and see, for a spirit doesn't have flesh and bones, as you see that I have."[109]

This revelation should the good news coming from our pulpits, because Jesus shows us that no matter how deep our spiritual suffering, no matter how agonizing our anguish, he shares it with us as our human partner. It doesn't mean that we won't experience our suffering; it means that we can never be overcome by it. Whether we are struck with soulful misery like Jesus in the garden, or suffer physical pain like Jesus on the cross, when we obediently accept our suffering as an act of participation in the life of the resurrected Jesus, we find a divine meaning that provides a sacred purpose beyond being some random event.

Saint Peter reminds us of this when he writes, "Beloved, think it not strange concerning the fiery trial which is to try you, as though some strange thing happened unto you: But rejoice, inasmuch as ye are partakers of Christ's sufferings; that, when his glory shall be revealed, you may be glad also with exceeding joy."[110]

Don't be fooled by churches that ignore suffering. Their teachings about a lifetime of prosperity, abundance and bounty have caused many Christians to end their life bitter, angry, afraid, or resentful when they were smacked down with unexpected suffering. We've all known Christians who went to their grave as

---

[109] Luke 24:38-39

[110] 1 Peter 4:12-13

a suffering soul asking why, after playing by all Gods rules, performing all the rituals, and doing all the right things; they were the innocent victims of a partial stroke or some other lingering illness.

Oswald Chambers, the inspiring author of "My Utmost for His Highest" once wrote, "We all know people who have been made much meaner and more irritable and more intolerable to live with by suffering: it is not right to say that all suffering perfects. It only perfects one type of person - the one who accepts the call of God in Christ Jesus."[111]

Q's

1. In terms of personal suffering, what is the will of God?
2. If God were faithful why would he allow his faithful to suffer?
3. Have you ever known someone who became bitter or resentful, as they grew older? What were the reasons? How did you deal with the person? Did they ever get better?
4. How does your church treat suffering? Is it a regular part of the sermon presentations? Does it facilitate small groups to discuss it? Would you like to hear more about biblical ways to live with suffering? Name some topics you'd be interested in.

---

[111] Taken from *The Place of Help* by Oswald Chambers © 1935 by Oswald Chambers Publications Association, Ltd. Used by permission of Discovery House, Grand Rapids MI, 49501. All rights reserved.

SUFFERING COMPASSION

Many times we confuse the compassion of Jesus with human compassion. Have you ever seen the picture of the young man with his head bowed down in shame or sorrow? Standing beside him is Jesus with his arm around the young man's shoulder giving him an embrace. The impression is that when we suffer, a sympathetic Jesus stands nearby to wrap us in his love, listen to our troubles and commiserate with us over our situation.

This view of God depicted in this popular illustration is certainly appealing. Like a strong brother, or understanding friend Jesus embraces us as if saying, "Steady, my son. This too shall pass." It's a sentimental portrait of Jesus that is a favorite among people who want a tender, emotion driven deity filled with love, harmony and heartfelt human compassion.

The biggest problem with this romantic picture is that it puts Jesus in the same category as every other god of compassion such as Allah or Quan-Yin. Each of these gods also offers their disciples divine compassion and sympathy. So if we use human compassion as a quality for choosing our God, then what is the difference between the three of them?

How is Jesus superior, and distinct?

Compassion is a human characteristic that expresses pity, mercy, or kindliness towards someone apart from us. While a person can express compassion for another human being, they cannot become that human being. They can euphemistically "feel their pain," but they cannot actually experience their pain. As humans, we are always separated by our flesh, and frustrated in our desire for an immersive loving union of sympathetic or empathetic inclusion.

But apart from extending our sympathy we are helpless to experience the suffering of someone else, although we may feel better for trying to understand it. The best that we can do is to pray for them. The best that we can say is, "I can only imagine what you're going through." Unfortunately they need more than our imagination to carry them through.

In the case of Jesus, he doesn't try to imagine what we are going through, he actually goes through it with us by a hypostatic union of his spirit with ours. In this way he does not stand apart, walk beside, or hover near us with his arm over our shoulder. Jesus does not sit upon a philosophic cloud at the right hand of God thinking good thoughts about us. He does not feel sorry for us, or live a fog of speculation wondering how we'll get through our suffering. Nor does he exist as the personification of some human trait called compassion, like the world's gods do. His divine compassion is found in the instantaneous internalization of our personal suffering right down to the nano-aspects of our human soul, brain synapses, and molecular biology.

The creamy portrayal of a sentimental Jesus doting over our emotional feelings is modern church salesmanship meant to attract consumers who seek a misty God of religious tenderness. It's no wonder that many Christians reach suffering in old age and struggle with their faith. When they reach out, and pray for God to be compassionate, nothing seems to happen. They were never taught that the compassion of Jesus comes from within, not from without. As such, they don't look inward to see that he is suffering with them, in them. For many it's too late, and they suffer alone.

Q's

1. How is human compassion different from divine compassion? How do we confuse the two?
2. Why would a person find human compassion to be more attractive than Jesus' compassion?
3. Do you believe that Jesus lives at the right hand of the Father somewhere, or inside you?
4. If you believe that he lives inside of you, where is that place? How do you get there?

SUFFERING WISELY

I am not suggesting that we all go out and find something to suffer about. There's no need for self-flagellation, there's plenty of suffering to go around. What I'm saying is that when we grow old we will be forced to suffer whether we want to or not. We must prepare for it now.

But how do we prepare? It's a rare case when a church teaches a theology of divine love that is experienced in, and through suffering. After all, preparing us to suffer hasn't been on the church's agenda for the last fifty years. Suffering doesn't seem relevant to people who think that suffering is what others do at the gym, or in some third world country. There is no converting the mind of a church that is satisfied in knowing what they think they know, and what they think they know is that the topic of suffering is of no interest to them.

Nevertheless, as each of us passes into the suffering of old age we will be confronted with the many hard realities that were not covered in their Bible studies and sermons. Have you ever heard a Christian say, "I take pleasure in weaknesses, in injuries, in necessities, in persecutions, in distresses, for Christ's sake?"[112] Mostly you hear them say, "It sucks to grow old," as they complain about every little ache, injustice, and pain.

Wise Christians behave differently. They look over the next hill and see what's on the other side. They ask, "Lord, show me

---

[112] 2 Corinthians 12:10

my end, what is the measure of my days. Let me know how frail I am."[113] And he responds from between the lines of Scripture that nothing of God is gained in comfort. They ask what are we to do? And his voice whispers that partnering with the man of suffering is the narrow gate that leads to salvation, and still waters.

How do we know this?

The proof occurred on a high mountaintop when God the Father showed the apostles that Jesus is the divine ruler of the supernatural, the natural, all law, life and death. "His face shone like the sun *(natural)*, and his garments became as white as the light *(supernatural)*. Behold, Moses *(law)* and Elijah *(resurrection)* appeared talking with him."[114] "A bright cloud *(eternal power)* overshadowed them. Behold, a voice came out of the cloud, saying, "This is my beloved Son, *(life)* in whom I am well pleased. Listen to him."[115]

What are we supposed to hear him say you ask? We are supposed to hear these words, "He who doesn't take his cross and follow after me, isn't worthy of me."[116]

No matter how much we think we know about Jesus, we cannot stand on the high mountaintop, and see him in all his glory until we trudge up the hill, and experience shared suffering with him. Soldiers understand this bond when they quote the words of the Saint Crispin's Day Speech in Shakespeare's play Henry V; "We few, we happy few, we band of brothers; For today

---

[113] Psalm 39:4
[114] Matthew 17:2
[115] Matthew 17:5
[116] Matthew 10:38

he that sheds his blood with me shall be my brother."

If we really want to listen to Jesus, we must take a deep breath of spiritual courage, and pick up our cross, and suffer as he suffers. We must learn from him everything that goes into that sacred practice. We must commit the time and energy that remains to us to study how he suffers in patience, courage, determination, wit, dignity, hope, forgiveness, kindness, and boldness.

A feel good religion, or a dismissive attitude about suffering will only take us so far. In old age our bravado will eventually break, like prisoners under a long grueling interrogation.

If we are going to enter the kingdom in style, we cannot act as if we have been treated unfairly, or punished by some invisible power in the last days of our life. Our faith must be that God has permitted whatever suffering we undergo for our good. Only by knowing this, can we suffer with a divine meaning, and a purpose that elevates us above the darkness of a cruel world that wants us to curse God and die.

Q's

1. Can a Christian prepare for suffering? What are some ways?
2. Describe the cross you bear. How do you manage to carry it day to day?
3. How could believing that Jesus actually suffers with you change your outlook?

SUFFERING SACRIFICE

One of the greatest blessings of growing old is that our playthings, pretends and passions are reduced to a point where we can finally concentrate on what's important. Through a gradual series of physical changes and mental awakenings our carnal desires and sins of pride begin to disappear. Some people see it as an occasion to rejoice, others a time of sadness. This is how Saint Paul saw it, "I count all things to be loss for the excellency of the knowledge of Christ Jesus, my Lord, for whom I suffered the loss of all things, and count them nothing but refuse, that I may gain Christ."[117]

You might ask, "What loss of all things? What will I suffer that I may gain Christ in old age?" To begin with you will lose your mind. No, I am not referring to Alzheimer's disease. What I am saying that your thoughts will begin to change. In old age we discover that ideologies we once held as vital, really aren't. Desires for sex, drugs and rock and roll don't seem as important. Ambitions for power or political control declines. We realize that our greatest earthly accomplishments are behind us. We gaze at an old photo and see that our looks are gone. We struggle to get up from a couch and know that we are losing our strength. We find that we can't use our favorite toys. Our motorcycles can't be driven because we've lost our balance, snow mobiles are too heavy to maneuver, airplanes are a danger to fly, golf clubs shouldn't be

---

[117] Philippians 3:8

swung because they threaten to rupture a disc, and scuba diving is way too risky. Ultimately we are reduced to the point where we have just one full time activity — trying to get to the bathroom before the bathroom gets to us.

Some people don't age well. Their identity remains in their past and they spend old age clinging to meaningless things they perceive as important. We only have to look at an aging politician still jockeying for power, a wealthy old woman still pursuing social importance, an old church know-it-all bossing everyone around, or the septuagenarian with a thirty-year-old girl friend. And so it goes.

With each advancing year some people will spend enormous energy and money fighting to keep their world from being stripped from their hands. But a wise Christian volunteers to let it all go, and chooses to walk with Jesus along the suffering old road to glory. They have no time to waste on foolish vanities or in weeping for themselves.

Q's

1. As you've aged, what things have you noticed that are different about your body, mind and soul?
2. How do you feel about growing older? What aspects of your life are you happy to give up? What things have been hard to let go?
3. What sins are you still clutching? How can you use growing older to help you release them?

SUFFERING SIGNIFICANCE

As we suffer the loss of all things, Jesus participates in our mental anguish and our physical pain to give our lives a new divine meaning and purpose. As we endure the grief, he allows us to touch his heart in a way that cannot be accomplished in any other fashion. In this manner we come to "know him, and the power of his resurrection, and the fellowship of his sufferings, becoming conformed to his death."[118] As much as we would like otherwise, there is no substitute for this suffering ordeal required by the sacred fire of the Holy Spirit.

While a prisoner in a Nazi concentration camp the noted Jewish psychiatrist Viktor E. Frankl observed that if a prisoner couldn't find a meaning to their senseless suffering or a purpose behind their random beatings they were far more likely to just give up and die in misery. Only in Jesus Christ can we find the meaning for our suffering and a purpose for the random beatings that life gives us. As the world's ultimate suffering sacrifice Jesus shows us the way that we are to partake in God's redeeming love. But we must share in the way — there is no free lunch or gratis grace. We must consent to participate in Jesus' divine life in a free-will partnership determined by him.

We can take comfort that our suffering is not a personal vendetta from God but an opportunity to help change our soul and the souls of those around us. The Father did not hold back

---

[118] Philippians 3:10

from his own Son when the salvation of the world was at stake, "Yet it pleased Yahweh to bruise him. He has caused him to suffer,"[119] so why should we expect him to hold back suffering from us when our world is at stake? In that truth we can find a meaning and purpose that will provide us a way to glorify God in our old age.

None of us wants to go out of this world as a decrepit old shell slumped in a wheel chair with a blanket on our lap. But if we can use it to help inspire people to change their lives and join us in heaven, then we can suffer with a smile knowing that our suffering is an act glorifying God.

Q's

1. What are the unbearable circumstances of your life? In what ways do you think that Jesus can take your present suffering and conform you to himself?
2. If your life is made unbearable by a lack of meaning and purpose, what can you do to obtain a meaning and purpose from God?
3. What meaning can you give to your sufferings? What purpose can you use them for?

---

[119] Isaiah 53:10

SUFFERING SAINTS

At the end of their lives many Christians will lose heart when God presents them with all of their flaws, mistakes, excesses and neurotic behavior they exhibited over their lifetime. Some will mourn, others will deny and many will weep that their life did not turn out as well as they expected.

As an example, a friend of mine who is a Bishop in his church shared a poignant story about an older woman, who came up to him saying,

"It's all a lie Bishop!"

"What do you mean?"

"My church promised that every day with Jesus would be sweeter than the day before. But I discovered that everyday with Jesus is harder than the day before."

My friend looked at the person and chuckled, "So you finally discovered the difference between what the Bible says about Jesus and what your church teaches?"

Like so many Christians, as the woman grew older she realized her life wasn't getting any better. She wondered where the God of promised miracles and abundance was. She grew frustrated not being able to reconcile the truth of her situation with the inflated guarantees and assurances of her clergy.

I don't blame intelligent spirit-led people who leave the church to find Jesus in their old age. Naturally, their fellow Christians will condemn or dismiss them as backsliders, outliers or hopeless heretics. But my Bible says, "The salvation of the righteous is from

Yahweh. He is their stronghold in the time of trouble. Yahweh helps them, and rescues them. He rescues them from the wicked, and saves them, because they have taken refuge in him."[120]

Naturally I'd like each of them to find a church of older people that teaches a realistic Christian understanding of life in old age. Nevertheless, I'm confident that Jesus will guide them along the journey to the new kingdom if they just continue to place their faith in his mercy with fear and trembling.[121]

The truth is that God has big shoulders and he is willing to accept the least of us who seeks his comfort and salvation with a contrite heart. In reality the God of creation is not limited to our sectarian theologies and doctrines. As a chastened Peter tells Cornelius, "Truly I perceive that God doesn't show favoritism; but in every nation he who fears him and works righteousness is acceptable to him."[122]

If you are feeling more and more estranged from church take heart, you are not alone. Find the Jesus living within you and sit with him each day. Learn to hear his voice. Trust that he will direct your steps. In the end, it will all boil down to just you and Jesus anyway.

Along the path keep your eyes open for others who feel alienated too. Listen for the voices of those who may have withdrawn also. Meet together to discuss your journeys of faith, unfaith, disappointments and even your skepticisms. Jesus promises that, "Where ever two or three gather in my name, there

---

[120] Psalm 37:39

[121] Philippians 2:12

[122] Acts 10:34-35

I am in their midst."[123] And he's a good listener. You may be surprised at what you discover.

Q's

1. Has your church ever let you down?
2. Is your present spiritual life content with the glowing promises of the modern church? If not, what have you done to fill the void?
3. Is there a middle ground between a God of wrath, and a God of tranquility?
4. Do you believe that you can go to heaven without going to church? If so, explain why and how.

[123] Matthew 18:20

THE SUFFERING CROSS

The modern Protestant church doesn't usually talk about suffering unless it's connected to a message on salvation. The rest of the time suffering is mostly ignored. Nevertheless, suffering is the divine requirement for Christian discipleship. Saint Paul explains why, "Because it has been granted to you on behalf of Christ, not only to believe in him, but also to suffer on his behalf."[124]

These days if you ask a Christian why Jesus suffered, the response will typically come in a rehearsed mantra, "So the world could be saved," which is partially correct. A fuller explanation is that he suffered to demonstrate *how* God loves us and *how* we are to love one another. If our salvation were only about his death, he could have allowed himself to die quickly and painlessly in any number of ways.

Why then did Jesus choose to suffer for as long and in the many aspects that he did? The answer is in the awkward truth that his soulful humiliation and physical pain gave us the standard of holy obedience if we want to be conduits of his divine love. It is the price we must pay to grow in grace and participate in his eternal life. "Then Jesus said to his disciples, "If anyone desires to come after me, let him deny himself, and take up his cross, and follow me."[125]

---

[124] Philippians 1:29
[125] Matthew 16:24

At this point, you might object saying that we cannot affect our own salvation through works,[126] which is true. But that is not what participatory sacrifice and suffering with Jesus are all about. What participatory suffering brings to us is the opportunity to obtain more of God's grace that expands our soul. In the modern translation, it is another way to "be blessed." Participatory suffering with Jesus is a voluntary act that brings a special unifying grace that opens our eyes to a greater apprehension of his divine love. It is an unexplainable blessing that draws us nearer to the heart of Jesus.

It is doubtful that Simon of Cyrene felt blessed when he was forced to pick up the cross of Jesus and made to suffer with him.[127] But if Simon had known that he was helping to support the savior of the world, he probably would have eagerly jumped in with both feet, and maybe even recruited a few more people to help him. Moreover, Simon's participation in the suffering walk of Jesus was not a random act thrown into the story for dramatic effect. It is God's way of showing us that a Christian is expected to participate in the ongoing salvation of the world. Meaning, that while Jesus died alone, he did not carry the entire weight of the cross of suffering alone. Someone was called to suffer with him and help carry his burden for part of the way. *Gasp!*

In old age, most of us will be forced to pick up the suffering cross of Christ. We can either accept it as a profound opportunity or reject it as being unfair. But either way, we will suffer in some or many forms. Thankfully, most of us only suffer the common

---

[126] Ephesians 2:8

[127] Matthew 27:32

headaches, worries, heartbreaks and pains of an old life. But if we are honest in our wish to carry the cross of Jesus, we must be prepared for whatever cross of suffering he allows.

Eventually, every Christian must get it into their head that Jesus' slow and painful crucifixion is not a symbolic one-time gesture that occurred two thousand years ago on a hilltop in Jerusalem by a really compassionate guy so that we could all live our lives in prosperity and skip merrily into heaven. We must give-up the ridiculous idea that Jesus suffered, sacrificed, and died to save us from suffering, sacrifice, and dying.

Jesus chose the suffering road over the course of his life to demonstrate the most profound love that God and a human being can experience on earth through a participatory union of temporal and divine suffering. As Saints Emeritus we have the opportunity to join in Jesus ongoing glorification of the Father by offering our suffering in an act of faithful obedience.

This is a difficult concept for Christians of the modern church who anticipate warm emotional "manna that comes down from heaven" to make them happy.[128] They expect all the benefits of heavenly citizenship without the price of naturalization. They reject the idea that their suffering can be turned into an act of divine grace by the power of the Holy Spirit. They deny that they have any role in their salvation. They dismiss that suffering and sacrifice has a divine meaning and purpose.

And so, when they discover that the drug of their contemporary religion can't stop their emotional pain, their

---

[128] Exodus 16:14

religious facade doesn't quell their fears, and their church membership can't overcome their lonely anguish, they are overwhelmed with soulful hollowness, which is greater suffering than all the others.

In the last years of their lives many Christians will clutch their Bibles or finger their beads, in an attempt to heal their suffering. They will grow sullen when it doesn't disappear. They will wonder what they've done to deserve this. They will become so focused looking upward to heaven for answers that they won't see the suffering cross of Jesus laying at their feet. Many will sit in the darkness of their rest homes, hospital rooms, and front parlors praying for the sweet embrace of death to take them quickly. They will ask for the suffering to stop at any price. And in the end it will be death they long for, not Jesus. Death will become their fixation, their most longed for idol, their ruling master and their blessed savior.

This is not how God envisions our life to end. This is not how it has to end.

Q's

1. What is the difference between being a fatalist in our suffering, and being faithful?
2. What are some ways that you can offer your everyday suffering to God?
3. Have you ever known a Christian who used their suffering as a way to participate in God's divine love?

PART FOUR

GROWING NEGLECT

"Now in those days, when the number of the disciples was multiplying, a complaint arose from the Hellenists against the Hebrews, because their widows were neglected in the daily service." - Acts 6:1

REFORMATION

There are three major reasons why the church doesn't address the spiritual issues of old age. The first is that it doesn't realize that there are any issues. The second is that older Christians don't think that they are old. The third is that the problems of older Christians are not the church's priority. To explain why they are not a priority we will need to look at how the Protestant church in America developed over the last hundred years, and how it drifted from its core obligation to provide comprehensive spiritual care to *all* souls entrusted to it.

In its abandonment of those central responsibilities we will also see that it shamefully outsourced the spiritual and emotional care of its olders to secular therapists, commercial businesses, and government programs. We will also learn that Protestant churches forgot their primary duty was to prepare everyone to meet Jesus at the hour of their death, especially in old age.

Don't assume that my complaints about the modern Protestant church are anti-church. They are no more anti-church than those of the Hellenists who complained about the church's neglect of their widows.[129] Nor are they any more anti-church than Martin Luther's complaints about the Vatican's treatment of the faithful. In the proper context of care and concern, complaints are simply requests for improvement and reform.

So it's not wrong to say that in the past eighty years Protestant churches developed a contrived blend of evangelistic opportunism, religious liberalism, and the invention of the gospel of prosperity to gain the favor of just one age group - the young. And instead of caring for all ages, they became a religious industry focused on competing for the time, money, and attention of the youth, and young families.

It's not wrong to point out that all of this competition for the attention of young people resulted in the abandonment of the spiritual needs of older people, and ultimately changed the church's spiritual charter, identity and mission. Moreover, it's very possible that this obsessive emphasis on winning the hearts and minds of the young, is one of the main reasons why twenty percent of all Americans now say that the Christian faith provides them no sense of meaning at all.[130]

If you're a zealous defender of your particular brand of church, my call for reform of the Protestant church, and its care of our senior citizens is not a request for you to give up your beloved preacher, cherished version of the Bible, familiar doctrines, personal theology, or attendance at your favorite weekly gathering.

---

[129] Acts 6:1

[130] www.pewforum.org/2018/11/20/where-americans-find-meaning-in-life/

I'm only inviting you to learn how evangelistic opportunism, religious liberalism, and the invention of the prosperity gospel resulted in the spiritual neglect of older people.

Q's

1. In what ways has your church made you spiritually ready for the hour of your death?
2. Do you believe that the spiritual care of olders is neglected in your church?
3. Make a list of three reforms you'd like your church to make regarding olders.
4. How can you help reform your church to make it a more suitable place for senior souls to thrive in?

"You shall rise up before the gray head, and honor the face of an old man." - Leviticus 19:32

THE DECLINE OF REVERANCE

There was a time when the people of God recognized that growing older was a sign of God's blessing and providence. It was his indication that a person was due some respect. But in the modern Protestant church, it is not the elderly who get the attention; it is the youth who are fawned over.

Much of this is driven by the church's cultural indoctrination by the media who portray older people as weak, indecisive, bumbling, stupid, or comical. Movies stereotype us as irritable, eccentric or foolish. Television programs present us as flakey, grumpy, capricious, or frisky.

The result is that in the marketplace of public opinion we are openly demeaned with slurs like a geezer, coot, codger, old-timer, or old bitty. Corporations patronize us by offering paltry discounts on meals and merchandise if we are willing to surrender our dignity to save a few pennies. "Must I show my membership card in the old people's association, or will the wrinkles on my face be enough proof?"

Without question, old age is hated in the Western culture and in the church of the Western culture where older members are the quiet victims of social stigmatization, and polite marginalization. Paraphrasing the words of Pastor Joe McKeever, a Southern Baptist minister who specializes in retirement ministry, *in the eyes of the church, senior citizens are sweet, saved, spiritual, selfless, senile, and sexless.*[131]

At best, we are viewed as a harmless collection of blue-haired women and knobby-kneed men with nothing to do, and all the time in the world to do it. We are expected to volunteer for church tasks that younger more "productive" members don't have time for. We are the gray-prey there to be exploited for our availability, and for the generous legacy gifts we are expected to leave the church after we die.

Beyond that, we are mostly invisible, alien creatures living in a world so foreign to young church leaders that they don't know what to do with us but to smile, and be polite. It never occurs to them that we have particular spiritual needs. They presume that a general Bible study, or a simplistic sermon on salvation will suffice in our old age.

What I am trying to make clear is that older people cannot expect ambitious young corporate clergy to cater to those of the 70s generation who now have saggy skin, arthritis, and hearing aids. Today's upward mobile executive pastors want to grow church attendance from the generation born since the '90s.

To be fair what can we expect from them? They can't know what they don't know. Anyone younger than fifty is still striving to find their meaning. Like the man once said, "all old people have been young, but no young people have been old."[132] Meaning, that clergy under the age of fifty are about as capable of

---

[131] http://joemckeever.com/wp/

[132] Attributed to Andrew Solomon.

showing an older person how to deal with their spiritual needs, as a blind person is capable of showing an artist how see the colors on a palette.

What does a forty-five-year-old know about the profound grief in watching your life fade away? How can a forty-year-old relate to the suffering found in loneliness, disappointment, and vanished success? What thirty-five-year-old can relate to hopelessness, guilts, or overwhelming regret? What twenty-something can conceive of daily sadness, irredeemable failures, scarring betrayals, or the depression that comes with seeing how your life didn't play out as you expected?

Nothing. But someday they will, if they live long enough.

Unfortunately, that doesn't help us now.

So what are we to do, we few, we proud, we happy band of Saints Emeritus?

Q's

1. Do you think that people in the congregation view you as an older person?
2. In what ways do they expect you to "act your age?"
3. Do you sense that you've become more isolated as you've aged?

"Listen to your father who gave you life, and don't despise your mother when she is old. Buy the truth, and don't sell it." - Proverbs 23:22-23

THE HISTORY OF NEGLECT

How did the Protestant church come to neglect its senior saints? In my version, it started at the turn of the twentieth century when three notable events occurred that generated the organization, motivation, and growth of commercially competitive churches jockeying for attendance and money.

The first was the Revenue Act of 1909, which granted tax immunity to churches and secular charitable organizations. The second was through Evangelicalism that taught the primary responsibility of every Christian was to engage their surrounding culture with the gospel. The third was the prominence of the Social Gospel movement that believed the individual was saved through religious engagement with society, and society was saved through government legislation created to fix national, state, and local problems based on biblical principles.

Hefty tax-free donations came pouring in which allowed churches to initiate strategic evangelical outreach campaigns to grow their membership, and enlarge their influence. Using new techniques of mass marketing, advertising and sales promotion copied from Madison Avenue, evangelists, revivalists, and major denominations began spreading their message. But the outreach to the American culture came at a transformational price. The American culture reached back sending waves of new members with modern consumer values into the church sanctuaries and seminaries.

By the 1950s, corporations had convinced Americans that by purchasing new products they could improve their life. Churches echoed that sentiment by claiming that the only product needed to enjoy the good life in this world, and the next was Jesus. There wasn't an ailment, heartache or financial problem that he couldn't cure. All it took was a personal declaration of faith, regular weekly attendance and a generous donation. Jesus went from being a heavenly healer to being a divine problem solver. What had once been the sober, sound, and solid biblical Protestant message of the previous generations was transformed into a culturally acceptable form of religious commercialism.

Over the next forty years mainline denominations retooled the stern deity of their grandfathers to create a new, and improved religious product that was softer, kinder and gentler on the user. They updated the language of their Bibles, modernized their worship practices, and replaced old church buildings with futuristic sanctuaries of sweeping architectural lines to reflect the new spirit of the times.

Pastors mimicked the style of popular entertainers. They included jokes, witty expressions, clever wordplays, homespun humor and rhyming clichés into their sermons. Good preaching was judged by the number of laughs the minister got, hands upraised in obedience, and contributions in the plate. Christian musicians combined rock and folk music to create a new sound called "Jesus music," which started replacing traditional hymns in popularity. Churches rushed to incorporate this music in a new invention called the "contemporary worship service." The idea was to sell the pleasures of church attendance to the coveted eighteen to thirty-four-year-old market segment.

Folks began showing up to worship wearing spandex, crop tops, tee shirts, fishing shorts, ripped jeans, flip-flops, and sneakers. The modern era of relaxed worship was introduced that continues to this day. The hardships of sailing on Noah's Ark were replaced with the comforts of sailing on the Good Ship Lollipop.

The fierce competition among churches for the "Me Generation"[133] divided Protestants into so many rival religious offerings that they branded themselves with emerging cultural agendas. Social justice, race advocacy, gay and lesbian lifestyles, radical feminism, gender-neutral language, environmentalism, and alternate forms of marriage characterized some of the new reasons for the spiritually inclined to join a church. At the other end of the spectrum, pulpit-pounding preachers raised their voices in biblical ire, and in dire condemnation of these activities hoping to attract people who were scandalized by the perceived radicalization of their traditional church or denomination.

The "soda wars" were on.

By the end of the twentieth century, despite their religious contortions, attendance figures of Protestant churches were in steep decline. Even leading Christian endeavors like the "Praise

---

[133] This is the name given to Baby Boomers by the writer Tom Wolfe.

and Worship" revolution, and the "Jesus Movement" were fading away. The situation became so bad that many of the mainline denominations had lost up to a third of their patrons.

When the new century rolled around, it was time to fix the problem of lagging church attendance. Enter what I call Protestantism 2.0. This time the inventors of the soft-spoken Jesus who ruled over the Age of Aquarius rebooted him as the Lord of the digital age. From the "superstar" of the 70s to the "rock star" of the new millennium, Jesus was presented as the God for a whole new breed of church that offered eternal youth in a non-establishment, non-doctrinal setting, with programs designed to affirm the illusion of a person's exceptional worth in the eyes of an indulgent God. The God of puritanical wrath and hellfire damnation was gone. He had repented of his past obsession with the devil, hell and unreasonable moral demands. And except in a few churches considered to be backwards by modern Protestant leaders, he became "Lord of all."

Throughout the country, hastily erected pre-fab metal buildings popped up. Auditoriums were built where worship took place on darkened stages equipped with computerized lighting, jumbotrons, massive sound speakers and dramatic effects. Weekly multi-media extravaganzas were set against digital backdrops of slow-motion effects, electronic clouds and high-energy music.

The white dove of Woodstock '69 fluttered in the rafters of the corporate sanctuary that worshiped an innocuous divinity unlikely to offend youthful sensitivities; a God that the young at heart could get along with, an amiable fellow with a backpack of blessings. He was a loving heart who wanted the best for everyone, a friendly, flexible, empathic God who yielded to everyone's emotional needs. He offered free moral clemency, blue jean reverence, safe faith, and universal self-esteem.

Borrowing language from Wall Street, a new breed of minister called the "executive pastor" invited attendees in business jargon to *hit the ground running, drill down, dive deep, think outside the box, move the needle, synergize, partner with him,* and *unpack* the scriptures.

More than one became a national celebrity writing self-help books filled with emotional therapy for lost souls drawn to flowery euphemisms, weepy stories, pliable religious demands, and continual promises of divine affirmation. In return, the faithful showed their allegiance by purchasing books, DVDs, tee shirts, jewelry, and wrist bracelets to "witness" their faith. Church parking lots overflowed with cars covered in crosses, church logos, stickers, and decals. It was the age of the bubble gum gospel, and purpose driven disciple.

It wouldn't be long before churches would be telling people to, "Like us on Facebook, subscribe to our YouTube channel, stream us on social media and download our mobile app to contribute online." In his wildest dreams, Johann Tetzel never imagined that religious sales could be this good.[134]

In the big steeple churches of the uptown elite where devotion to Saint Laurent took place, the self-absorbed aristocracy closed their eyes, held their nose, and ignored the sea change taking place in Protestant worship, and community life. They did so at their own peril.

---

[134] The zealous indulgence seller of the Middle Ages who was tasked with raising money to build Saint Peter's Basilica in Rome.

Ironically, in the massive effort to provide for every conceivable youth driven satisfaction, Protestant churches virtually eliminated the discipline, temperance, suffering, sacrifice, and sacred devotion that serious seekers of salvation were drawn to the cross for. Discarded in the rush to manufacture a mood-based faith for easy consumption were any requirements for soulful introspection, and obedient piety. Sacrifice, suffering, humility, prudence, abstinence, temperance, and chastity had all been traded for entrepreneurial opportunism, childish distractions, clownish amusements, tawdry showmanship, and electronic irreverence geared to the capricious wishes of youth.

In the past few years, Jesus was updated once again and downloaded in Protestantism 3.0 as a tender hyper-aware millennial staying in touch with his church through social media. People attending a Protestantism 3.0 congregation will *immerse* themselves in the Word like members of a synchronized swim team. They will hear about the joys of membership from gospel cheerleaders who are excited to be excited about being excited. They will be washed in a teaching we might call "spiritual affirmation," where Jesus' humanitarianism, God's desire for coexistence, and his unconditional tolerance are presented as the highest forms of social virtue.

As people grew older, many wearied of listening to dumbed-down narratives preoccupied with self, a litany of Christian cliché's meant for children, and sermonic pep talks from a pastor perched atop a bar stool in designer jeans trying to look cool. They knew that something was wrong. Their life was nothing like what the pastor was saying. Their soul was anything but joyful.

Something had changed about their world, and they knew it. Something deep inside was aching, and nobody was talking about it.

Ironically, these were the very same people who had once championed the new flavor of church meant for the tastes of the young. But in the disco age leading to the World Wide Web, it never occurred to them that they were creating a spiritual atmosphere that would eventually lead them out the door. They never imagined that their religious reengineering would result in being separated from the church of eternal youth that they had helped build. They had always assumed that a perpetually young generational church was how God meant church to be. Maybe it is for teens and young families, but not for mature adults.

Given time, they realized that there was no place to go and hear a grownup message of spiritual relevance for people their age. There was no church offering an environment to socialize and share the life of hardship experienced by an older person. So they simply accepted their fate, turned off their hearing aids, grew gray in the pews, volunteered to help out where they could, or just faded away from church altogether; the victims of their own adolescent decisions.

Q's

1. Have you ever placed a religious sticker on your car, or worn a piece of apparel with a Christian saying on it? Explain why or why not.
2. Has your church adopted any of youth driven religious practices over the last thirty years? What are they?
3. Does your church offer a separate worship service for older people? If so, how is the message different?
4. If Jesus only lived to the age of thirty-three, how can he understand the problems of an older person?

"When they had crucified him, they divided his clothing among them, casting lots, and they sat and watched him there." - Matthew 27:35-36

THE SQUEEZE PLAY

A brief look at the nature of the modern church will help to explain why older people were squeezed out of the church priorities. You probably have your own definition of what church is, but one thing we should all agree on is that church is a business. To illustrate, let's say that the major franchises of Christianity are the Roman Catholics, the Orthodox, and the Protestants. Think of them being like three different beverage companies. The Roman Church offering coffee, the Orthodox Church offering tea, and the Protestant Church offering soda.

Protestantism is a relatively new understanding of the Bible that provides people a different beverage experience. It's available in hundreds of theological flavors. We might call the Baptists Root Beer, Presbyterians Lemon-lime, Methodists Strawberry, Pentecostals Cherry, Episcopalians Grape, Lutherans Cola, and so forth. And like any soda company, each Protestant church sells its theological product to stay in business.

While they may think that they are the only authentic flavor approved by God, and they may believe that they are above crass commercialism, at the heart of every Protestant denomination or nondenominational church, it's not their doctrine, theology,

Bible translation or faith principles that they have in common; it's their ongoing need to sell their brand of Protestantism to raise money.

So what? We know that from the earliest times church congregations collected money. Here's what.

When modern Protestants form a church, it usually begins with two or three believers gathered in someone's living room. At first, they pool their money to pay for the refreshments and incidentals. In time the number of people grows, and the founders decide it will be more comfortable if they meet in a larger place like a conference room. Again, they pool their money. But eventually more and more people start coming. Which is a good thing, but they will need more refreshments, and maybe a few additional Bibles. Soon, the gathering reaches a point where they want their own church campus, or sanctuary. But the question of how they'll finance the rent, furniture, heat, electricity, insurance, etc., becomes an issue. So, they conduct a holy huddle, and decide that according to Malachi 3:7-12 tithing is a biblical mandate, and a measure of a person's obedience to God. Therefore, the time has come for all attendees to be highly obedient to God.

Just about then, one of the rich members of the congregation decides to show her obedience with a seven-figure financial donation. But her accountant asks if her contribution will be tax deductible. Suddenly, the need to be able to provide tax-deductible donations becomes very important. And here is arguably the single biggest reason why the modern Protestant church varies from that of the New Testament. The founders decide to organize a formal business corporation to manage the church business, and encourage more endowments, and contributions. It will not be just any kind of Business Corporation; it will be a non-profit business corporation with all of the benefits of an IRS tax-deductible 501(c) 3 c. status.

But in order to properly incorporate, the group will need to form a board, and find a lawyer to file the paperwork. Then someone on the board will say that the woman's very generous seven-figure gift should be used to erect a sanctuary. Of course that will mean locating a realtor to purchase the property, an architect to draw up plans for the sanctuary, a banker to float a construction loan, a contractor to build it, and a part-time minister to make it all official. Happily, as it turns out, one of the members is an architect, another is a realtor, another is an attorney, another is a banker, another has property to sell, another is a contractor, and one of them always wanted to be a preacher.

Every first year business student learns that the greater success a business has, the more it must work to maintain it. So, from the moment our small gathering becomes successful enough to break ground on their new sanctuary, the primary business of their church will become maintaining that success. Every leadership effort will be measured against the ledger of sustainability. Every program, event, and gathering will be weighed against its financial loss or profit. In many cases, if any preaching, teaching or doctrinal position threatens the loss of their 501 (c) 3 IRS tax status, it will be modified or suppressed.

Soon the accumulation of money will be the single major concern of the small group that started with the noblest of religious intentions. They will raise it, spend it, take loans against it, give updates about it, worry about it, and finally build a ceremonial bonfire to celebrate the burning of their mortgage, only to turn around and announce a new building expansion program. All the time they may pretend to be above seeking "filthy lucre" in their capital campaigns, but everyone knows that their church is a business that must attract fresh money, and new customers by offering their particular flavor of "soda" to the spiritually inclined.

Again, so what? There is nothing wrong with a church raising money. Just as a soda company sells root beer to pay their overhead, the incorporated church sells its flavor of Jesus Christ. Just as a soda company sees the world as a giant marketplace of potential customers, so does the incorporated church. The main difference is that the incorporated church believes that it has a divine mission to go into the world, and make consumers of their particular flavor of Jesus.

To that end churches advertise the kind of personal satisfaction their flavor of Jesus offers. Some claim that their religious formula is never watered down. Others say that their religious ingredients include the proper Bible translation, or the correct prayer language. Many declare that their particular soda flavor provides the user with an uncompromising Word of God, or the unvarnished truth about the Scriptures. Some even assert that their soda flavor has a miraculous connection to God that virtually guarantees the consumer exclusive admission into heaven.

To enhance their appeal, churches often present a variety of social packages meant to attract and keep customers. Some sell their catalogue of "family friendly" programs and activities. Others subtly emphasize the status or wealth of the person you'll rub elbows with. Many tout their importance as the city's oldest church, or a church of the founding fathers, or a church of the abolitionists, or a church of freed slaves, or a church of the freed LGBTQ. More than one church offers a form of religious militancy through a broad menu of ongoing social activism programs. Some churches highlight their use of gender-neutral pronouns, or an inclusive language Bible. Others point to their LGBTQ ministers and female priests as examples of enlightened Christianity. Many promote the language they use, culture they express or color of skin as reasons for attending. From touting a special method of baptism, to promoting conservative or liberal views, every church markets its religious specialty to a specific type of consumer.

Anyone who thinks that their church is above tailoring their spiritual flavor to a specific market segment has probably never seen a billboard out in front of their church advertising Vacation Bible School, or some cute message appealing to the passerby. In some places you might see a rainbow flag, or "Join Us" banner flying out front of the sanctuary. And if you still don't believe that your church isn't in the business of marketing its product through sales, you've probably never heard the following words uttered from your pulpit, "And remember to bring someone you know to worship next Sunday."

We might ask why Protestant churches over the last century felt the need to redesign themselves in an effort to attract, and charm souls for Jesus. After all, as Dietrich Bonhoeffer once pointed out, "Jesus himself did not try to convert the two thieves on the cross; he waited until one of them turned to him."[135]

But we'd be missing the point. Churches and denominations don't want people to attend any old church; they want them to attend their church. Who's ever heard of the Methodists sending missionaries out to convert people to join a Presbyterian Church? What Episcopalian congregation prays for the success of the Fundamentalist Church down the street? What Lutheran church sends money to roof the classroom of a Church of Christ congregation? Have you ever seen an advertisement in the newspaper where the Baptist's say, "We don't care where you go to church. Just go to church?"

Which begs two questions; what makes any of these groups think that they have a better product to offer than any other church? What makes them think they are in competition for membership?

As we shall see, the focus on the business of the church, the intensity of religious competition between churches, and the clamor to attract young people, directly impacted how churches came to view, and treat their elderly.

---

[135] Letters and Papers from Prison, Touchstone, July 1, 1997.

Q's

1. What exactly is the church? Is it an institution that Jesus founded, a building we worship in, the religion we believe, or the people who gather together? Is it something more? Is it something else?
2. Does your church spend most of its money taking care of the poor people in the congregation, or poor people outside the congregation?
3. Has there ever been an appeal in your church for money to purchase programs, Bible studies, or equipment for the spiritual welfare of the elderly?
4. Has your church ever recommended that people attend another church for their spiritual care? Why, or why not?
5. Do you think that pastoral alliances, and an occasional ecumenical service are what Jesus meant when he prayed to the Father, "that they may be one, even as we are."[136]
6. What flavor of Protestant soda does your church serve? How is it different or better than other churches?

---

[136] John 17:11b

"Strangers have devoured his strength, and he doesn't realize it. Indeed, gray hairs are here and there on him, and he doesn't realize it." - Hosea 7:9

THE GRAND INFATUATION

So what does this short history of the business of the incorporated Protestant church in America say to us? It says that the primary marketing goal of our churches over the past fifty years has been to capture one particular religious customer - the youth. It explains why churches began adjusting their traditional understandings of Jesus. It tells us why there has been continual experimenting with different expressions of belief and worship styles. It answers why churches have seen no reason to invest in the spiritual development of senior citizens, and why they have ignored the growing market demographic of older adults. It's not that the church has been cruel to older people; it has just been indifferent, and blind to their needs.

Even now, the central planners of the corporate Protestant churches are pursuing the upcoming generations of Y and Z. They are spending big dollars and countless hours running back and forth to conferences, luncheons, and seminars discussing methods of how to win the youth,[137] and ways to support young families.[138]

---

[137] Answers in Genesis Conference, https://www.sharefaith.com/blog /2015/05/ top-30-christian-conferences-2015-2016/

[138] D6 Conference, https://www.sharefaith.com/blog/2015/05/top-30-christian-conferences-2015-2016/

They are talking about the ever-growing importance of electronic technicians who manage the mega worship spectacles.[139] Perhaps the biggest fuss is about the latest trend in Christian music.[140]

Not one of the significant church conferences for 2018 listed on the Share Faith website[141] concerned the spiritual development or needs of people over fifty. Nothing on the agenda indicated that they would discuss the real future of the church, which is the flooding growth of people older than fifty. Why? Because despite the preponderance of demographic evidence that America is rapidly aging, the corporate church remains stuck on the idea that it's only about the youth.

But they are making a big mistake.

First, the Baby Boomers (55+) are already the most significant market demographic in America, and by 2035, people over sixty-five will outnumber all of the youth in the United States. Jonathan Vespa, a demographer with the U.S. Census Bureau, put it this way, "The aging of baby boomers means that within a couple of decades, older people are projected to outnumber children for the first time in U.S. history."[142]

If enlightened church planners actually want to see substantial

---

[139] FILO Conference, Sound and Media Tech Conference. Conferencehttps://www.sharefaith.com/blog/2015/05/top-30-christian-conferences-2015-2016/

[140] Christian Musician Summit, Immerse Conference, https://www.sharefaith.com/blog/ 2015/05/top-30-christian-conferences-2015-2016/

[141] www.sharefaith.com/blog/2015/05/top-30-christian-conferences-2015-2016/

[142] "Older People Projected to Outnumber Children for First Time in U.S. History," March 13, 2018 Release Number CB18-4. U.S. Census Bureau.

church growth in the future, they should design a church that meets the spiritual needs of the elderly. They will have to admit that all of their juvenile hype is not in sync with the current or future demographics of the nation.

It will be interesting to see if they will retool their ministry efforts, and begin serious outreach to older Americans. I hope so. But it will take an inspired plan with age capable adults to shepherd it. Meanwhile, millions of people will keep aging without much attention from a church that is still seeking the approval of the youth.

Q's

1. Would you say that there are more people over fifty, or younger than fifty in your church? Has your church ever taken a census? What would it learn from the results?
2. Having youth in a congregation is essential. In what ways do you feel that your church has catered to their needs at the expense of older members?
3. Can a church present a single biblical message during Sunday worship that speaks to the spiritual needs of youths, young adults, the middle-aged, and senior citizens in the congregation?

PART FIVE

GROWING UP

A DECLARATION

As we continue to grow old there is a wave of white-capped olders swelling the church pews. We are the faithful who have been the bulwark of the church for the past half-century or more. We have funded, planned, and built the structures, programs, and retreat centers that the church enjoys today. We have led youth groups and mission trips. We have faithfully attended worship services, (even though for many of us it has become as difficult to hobble from the church parking lot into the sanctuary as an agonizing pilgrimage up the steps of the Scala Sancta.) And we wonder why we didn't put in more ramps and handicapped parking spots when we had the chance.

In their hurry to ensure that young families are having fun, making friends and doing the busy work of the church, the leadership forgets that we have already participated in countless mission trips, Bible studies and service programs. Forgotten too are the endless hours of labor we have donated. Instead, when the pastor formulates his sermon on Christian discipleship, we are lumped in with the children, youth, teens and young families.

They don't consider that we no longer need sermons about salvation; we accepted Jesus forty years ago. We don't require moral messages on family life; we've raised our families. We don't want lectures on marriage; we've been married for decades, or are now widows or widowers.

Week after week, we endure Bible studies geared for people still in their formative learning years. Most of us have been living a life of Christian virtue and moral living longer than most of the younger members have been alive. Nevertheless, what we get from the pulpit is the same rehash of the gospel message we've already memorized, internalized, and evangelized for most of our life.

We have deposited our lives into our church like a 401K plan, and now it's time we receive our golden parachute. It's time to get our spiritual benefits package. What might those be? Among those that I'd like to see would be a church that devoted to preaching and learning about the spiritual changes that take place during aging. A church that takes time to comprehend the complexities of growing old and has a preaching climate that routinely presents Biblical topics relevant to older people who, like Saint Paul, actually *see* their day of departure coming. I'd especially like to see a respectful clergy who don't trivialize old age with cute little quips from the pulpit.

In my view, it could all start with an inspired leadership that stops seeing the elderly as objects of curiosity or as a subgroup of an alien life form. As one example, I recall reading the story of a youth minister who was sent by his church on a field trip to visit a local rest home. He wasn't sure what to expect, but he was astounded when he discovered that the people living there were just like him, only older. He was so excited that he felt compelled to write a report about his experience outlining four ways that a "gospel-centered ministry" (whatever that is) could care for the elderly. What was clear in reading his suggestions was that because of his youth he was unable to connect with older people based on experience, so he viewed them as distant objects to sympathize, study, dissect and document. While the observations of a young minister about older people may provide an excellent foundation for his pastoral ministry in forty years, what a graying church needs right now are mature and experienced spiritual guides who can conduct studied in-reach to older adults on a full time basis.

Unfortunately, in the current milieu of millennial madness, this seems to be too much to ask of a clergy still competing for the attention of the young. It's a challenge for them to realize that grab rails and ramps are not a sign of weakness. They don't get the fact that standing for thirty minutes of praise music is tough for most olders. It's even harder to get them to stop humiliating older people by singling them out by saying insensitive things like, "If you are too old, weak, decrepit, faltering, or shaky to stand, you may sit down with the rest of the unworthy."

The issue of a church accommodating and providing for the aging saints is not an either-or proposition. It is a both-and proposal. It is one that can, and should be met in balance. The fifty-year pendulum of the church's focus on the youth has created such a vast sucking spiritual vacuum for older people that many have simply vanished from the pews to join the church of Saint Dunne — the patron saint of those who are done with church.

We can't blame them. It's not that they didn't try to hang with the edgy youth, and the cool vibes. They patiently indulged the efforts of their clergy hoping to energize the vitality and attendance of younger people. They wanted their beloved church to thrive and survive. Like any good parent, they sacrificed their own spiritual needs for those of their children, and accepted the dwindling spiritual attention they received. Which eventually came in the form of a sympathetic home visit from an associate pastor, or a well-intentioned pat on the arm from a buzz cut staff member.

All along, they kidded themselves into thinking that the spiritual milk coming from their pulpits would provide them with strength in old age. But after the years passed without any meaningful spiritual notice, they realized that they had been relegated to the status of adorable relics to be trotted out once a year for recognition on their birthday or anniversary. In the end, they discovered that were on their own to glean whatever spiritual solace they could from the activities of a church that had passed them by.

The prolific Presbyterian pastor George Buttrick once compared the gathering of the faithful to the assembling of an orchestra. Why then, do so many churches overlook the largest section of their band?

Q's

1. A thriving congregation is not determined by size, but by effectiveness. How effective has your church been in meeting the spiritual needs of older people?
2. Is your congregation turning into a church of people over fifty? Do you anticipate that it will still be around in thirty years? If so, how?
3. Is it right to throw older people under the bus so that the church can focus on recruiting younger people in the hopes of surviving?

4. Do you think that the goal of a church should be survival at any price, or can a church community be allowed to dwindle out?
5. What suggestions could you offer to help make your church more focused on the spiritual care of people older than fifty?

THE RECLAMATION

A two-thousand-year-old church should have the maturity, experience, and resources to do more than pay prayerful lip service to the suffering of its olders, or to outsource them to secular caregivers. Somewhere in the network of Christianity, there must be men and women capable of formulating a theology of suffering to prepare a person for their transition from youthful vibrancy to aging vacancy.

It's time for serious Protestant clergy to present topics of Christian suffering that teach us why we can depend upon a God who suffers with us. Surely it would lessen the shock for the youth as they grow older, and it would help the elderly as they entered the shadows of the valley of their own death.

If you think that your church is different, look around the foyer for any Bible-based literature, small group studies or continuing education programs focused on shaping the congregation to cope with the silent changes that will move them from the comforts of their home to the confines of a rest home.

Please don't confuse part-time church activities overseen by someone with a title like "Director of Senior Fellowship" or "Senior Adult Coordinator" as providing intentionally structured study programs, sermons or worship for the relevant training required for spiritual aging.

Ministers preaching that Christianity is a lifelong gospel jubilee ending with, "and they all lived happily ever after," are tragically disingenuous and harmful to all of us. How many times does Jesus have to say, "If anyone desires to come after me, let him deny himself, take up his cross, and follow me," before they get it?

Long ago, the church considered suffering as the central theme in the life of Jesus. It was the stated expectation of his followers. Every book of the Bible addressed it. Church fathers and theologians wrote about it. And Reformers emphasized it. It's time to get back to the teachings and practice of sacrifice and suffering. It's time for churches to understand that no one can pick up their cross and follow Jesus when they are invited to come into the sanctuary holding a hot latte in one hand.

Q's

1. Why should the church get back to the teaching, and practice of sacrifice and suffering?
2. In what ways does your church teach you the need to sacrifice or suffer?
3. Make a list of four things you would hate to sacrifice in old age.
4. Make a list of three ways you would hate to suffer in old age.
5. Explain how you would handle the sacrifice, and suffering you listed in questions three and four.

APPLICATIONS

Perhaps you attend a church where the majority is older than fifty. Maybe they all grew up together. They're probably not even aware that they are older. It's place where people are used to hearing comfortable sermons about God's children, the blessings of belonging to a church family, and the love of Jesus. The congregation looks forward to the benediction so that they can socialize on the patio with coffee, donuts and breakfast tacos. Grandma and grandpa like to talk about their grandchildren, and swell with pride when little Sally runs to the front of the sanctuary to listen to a children's sermon with one other kid.

You belong to a congregation that was raised during the radical age of Protestant change in America. They probably don't realize that the winsome message they've heard ever since their youth, with its undeveloped gospel, and sweet musical milk, cannot sustain their soul as they age. It hasn't occurred to anyone that listening to serene sermons about symbols of grace, and practicing a flannel board faith is spiritual food for teenagers. They don't know that they need crafted sermons of wisdom designed to strengthen their souls, sooth their fears, explain their sufferings, and teach them the courage to age. No one has told them that they require the rich cream of the sacred served in a holy ambiance of unhurried prayer.

The Bible tells us that there is a season for everything. There is a time for the God of our youth, and a time for the God of old age. He has never changed, but we have. If you are older than fifty, it's time to update your personal understanding about your spiritual needs. It's the moment when you must decide the role your church should play in your life. Thankfully, you have reached the age where you can help reform your church's worship, scripture studies, sermons, attitudes, and community life to satisfy the requirements of people living in the final season of their lives.

What we saw illustrated in the stories of Deacon Tim, Reverend Jackson and Ms. Joan is that millions of souls have not been able to survive on the teachings of a modern faith that ignores the suffering trials of age. Without being challenged to embody Christ's sacrifice and suffering, there was little strength left in their souls to sustain them when they became disillusion in old age. They gave up, shriveled up, and finished up symbolically waving a bony fist at an empty sky.

The good-time message of the painless gospel didn't prepare them to become heartbroken shut-ins, terminally ill patients, or vomiting geriatrics. There was no spiritual training offered in their youth to equip them for solitary confinement in a bed. The gospel of sociability didn't teach them how to deal with the realities of an isolated life. The promise of high expectations faded when they were placed next to a window overlooking a parking lot for twelve hours a day.

When the preachers and theologians of the last century rejected physical and mental suffering as a fundamental truth of Christian living, they eliminated a primary reason why people need a savior. Instead of establishing training centers for how people can endure suffering across the spectrum of their life, churches became social country clubs offering seekers a religious menu promising comfort and affluence.

You might ask why they abandoned the call for suffering? It's simple; people don't want to suffer. And if that meant offering a pain-free gospel to attract their attention, then the end justified the means. Soon churches were selling a seat in the sanctuary of blissful family life. At about that same time many American churches lost their salt. "Foolish Galatians, who has bewitched you not to obey the truth, before whose eyes Jesus Christ was openly set forth among you as crucified?"[143]

Deacon Tim, Reverend Jackson, and Ms. Joan all grew up in the church of human happiness that imagined older people spending their golden years in sunny Florida, strolling barefoot along a sandy beach with their sexy sixty-something partner while smirking about their life's accomplishments, and toasting each other over a glass of wine at poolside. But most churchgoers will face their last years with medical problems, unexpected bills, dwindling income and limited physicality.

It's not surprising that Deacon Tim, Reverend Jackson and Ms. Joan, grew isolated, angry, and depressed when confronted by the tsunami of spiritual suffering that aging brought them. They trusted the rites, rituals, doctrines, and feel good messages of their prosperity parish. Their church never taught them how life really ends, spiritually prepared them with ways to deal with its painful reality.

---

[143] Galatians 3:1

Q's

1. What problems do you face as you grow older?
2. How do you envision your life during your last years?
3. Are you preparing for old age, or will you deal with it when you get there?
4. At what age will you "get there?"
5. Have you ever taken a trip, and not packed for the destination? What happened?

THE CALLING

In a church that recognizes the call for geriatric ministry, aging must be a full-time topic of interest. The church will specialize in biblical ways to understand it, and offer a practical means for Christians to live with it. Members will be sensitized to aging's reality, and taught biblical methods to understand the sufferings and pains of growing older.

Depending upon the size of the church, it should split its congregation into those who are older than fifty, and those who are younger. Under the current configuration of most Protestant churches, both age groups are expected to worship in a sort of frontier-style one-room schoolhouse where everyone from kids to seniors attends the service. Using this outdated approach, the two age groups cannot be ministered to correctly, or at the appropriate levels of spiritual understanding. Nobody benefits by listening to a one size fits most sermon. A separate gathering should be established for those over fifty that doesn't allow younger men and women or their families to attend.

For example, depending on the size of the church, the senior service could be held in a separate building where a sanctuary would be configured to have more space devoted to wheelchairs and walkers. Hearing devices would be available and acoustics would be tuned for diminished hearing. Large print Bibles, programs and literature would be incorporated to allow greater ease for the older congregation to follow the service. The expectation of standing, sitting or kneeling throughout the service would be abolished. Music would be geared to the tastes of an older group.

The senior gathering would have its own mission statement, and budget offerings would be specifically designated for it. Predictably, its leaders would be people no younger than fifty. Its weekly gathering would consist of a combination worship and healing service where, in addition to elements such as prayer, communion, music and readings, all members of the congregation would be anointed with oil, and receive the laying on of hands.

Benedictions, rituals, and the entire spiritual mindset would be geared towards the acknowledgement of how Christ's suffering is our model for spiritual sustainability. In the absence of children and young adults, sermons and programs could be presented on mature topics of spiritual concern in a setting exclusively designed for older people. On major occasions such as Easter and Christmas, the older and younger services could be combined for a special service.

Don't think that it will be enough to modify the existing church worship service with a few patronizing items, and token sermons for grandma and grandpa. Spiritual topics and the language used during sermons of interest to elders are not rated PG. What I am suggesting is the establishment of an entirely new kind of church service, or satellite community, either on or off the campus that consists exclusively of members over fifty.

Q's

1. Why would dividing your church into two separate age groups benefit everyone's spiritual growth?
2. What religious elements would benefit a church of people over fifty?
3. What spiritual topics would you appreciate being addressed in a church for people over fifty?

THE RECALLING

Perhaps we will have to recall older ministers who will come out of retirement and lead the new church of the Saints Emeritus. We will need a suffering person who understands the spiritual challenges of old age. We may have to search high and low for a wise teacher who can build a curriculum for older people to follow. We may even wonder if God has groomed prophetic guides who have lived long enough to share biblical insight, and spiritual experiences from the perspective of age. It may not be easy to find inspired Christian leaders who can or want to teach us how to grow old. It's hard to say if God will send us older leaders with a vision for the elderly, who can help us study the lives of the great older saints in the Bible, who were more richly blessed by God in the last years of their lives than they were during their younger years.

Here are a few models of older people of faith that an older minister might preach about and teach Bible studies on.

- Moses was eighty, and Aaron eighty-three when God called them to speak to Pharaoh.[144]
- Abraham was ninety-nine when he suffered the price of a divine bond through circumcision.[145]
- Sarah was ninety at Isaac's birth.[146]

---

[144] Exodus 7:7

[145] Genesis 17:11

[146] Genesis 18:13

- Simeon was in his eighties before he received a smile from Jesus.[147]
- Anna was about eighty-four before she beheld the face of Jesus.[148]
- Zacharias and Elisabeth were well advanced in years when their son John the Baptizer was born.[149]
- Isaiah died an old man after prophesying for more than sixty-four years.
- Deborah, the judge and prophetess, lived into her late sixties.[150]
- Rahab was fifty years old when she protected the spies sent by Joshua.[151]
- St. Paul shared his message until his martyrdom at about the age of sixty-five.[152]
- St. Peter labored for Jesus until his crucifixion at about the age of sixty-seven.[153]
- St. John wrote his divine accounts until he was about one hundred.[154]

These saints lived during a time when there were no corner

---

[147] Luke 2:25-32
[148] Luke 2:37b
[149] Luke 1:13
[150] https://www.chabad.org/library/article_cdo/aid/112050/jewish/The-Prophetess-Deborah.htm
[151] https://www.geni.com/people/Rahab/6000000002689040201
[152] https://www.reference.com/world-view/old-apostle-paul-died-d738346c9cfd066c
[153] http://www.newadvent.org/cathen/11744a.htm
[154] http://www.newadvent.org/cathen/08492a.htm

drug stores, no mobility scooters, no Medicare, and no emergency hospitals, just their complete dependence upon God, total faith in his promises, and a burning desire to serve him until their last breath. And these are just some of the models of senior faith that we can learn from, and emulate in the days that remain before us.

Q's

1. How did the older saints in the Bible react to God's calling?
2. How did their life change?
3. How was each one used by God?
4. What types of mental or physical suffering do you think they experienced?
5. Has God called you to provide a special service in old age? How did he prepare you for it?
6. Would you like God to call you? If so, what do you think he would want you to do?

PART SIX

GROWING GRACE

"For you, brothers, were called for freedom. Only don't use your freedom for gain to the flesh, but through love be servants to one another." - Galatians 5:13

WHAT CAN WE DO?

Not everything about old age is horrible. Some of its best aspects are in the discovery that we no longer have to impress anybody, or get the approval of someone else. We are free to be exactly who we are. No one can rule our life, except the doctors and politicians who govern our healthcare, and social security.

We can get up when we want, wear what we want and talk to whom we wish. We don't have to wear a business suit, skirt or professional attire. We can go to church in loud Hawaiian shirts and floral muumuus; baggy jogging pants or bib overalls. Or, we don't have to church at all, and go fishing instead. We can let our tummy lap over our belt or go without makeup. Nobody cares.

But seriously, in old age we experience a special kind of wisdom born from a lifetime of surviving a dangerous world. We find contentment when reading the Book of Proverbs knowing that we couldn't have said it better ourselves. Even more satisfying is the fact that we now realize that we have been given additional time by God to prepare our souls for the goal of the prize awaiting us in heaven. As a paratrooper might say, "we are just sixty seconds away from the drop zone, waiting for the green light to come on."

I'm sure that you have your own ideas about the world we'll find the moment we take our last breath and open our eyes. Whether you see heaven as just the first door to an infinite universe, the gateway to a divine multiverse, a celestial theme park, a city where the streets are paved with gold, or something altogether different, heaven will be an existence more breathtaking than our wildest imaginations can conceive.

For the first time we will meet Jesus face to face, and learn from his own lips the person we were created to be. We will be given a personal tour of the custom tailored "room" he specially designed for us. He will answer our questions as he explains "the rest of the scriptures," and what all of the madness of this world was about.

We will thank the angels that looked over us, and meet the archangels who serve God to manage all of existence. We will hug every saint in the cloud of witnesses, and share stories, and joy, and praises of God's salvation with all of the elect. We may even learn that there are more aspects of reality yet to be revealed. Maybe Jesus will unveil what the other ninety-percent of our brain was made to do. Maybe there will be new physical or mental senses, vibrant color spectrums, molecular frequencies, sound harmonics, and other wonders to enjoy.

So on those days when you are feeling old and tired, discouraged or fearful, keep in mind that the glory of God in heaven is our destination. And no matter what suffering or sacrifice we experience along the way, remember that Jesus says, "Don't let your heart be troubled. Believe in God. Believe also in me. In my Father's house are many rooms. If it weren't so, I would have told you. I am going to prepare a place for you. If I go and prepare a place for you, I will come again, and will receive you to myself; that where I am, you may be there also."[155]

Q's

1. What is the best part of your old age?
2. Why do you suppose many people don't figure out the obvious until they are older?
3. Do you have a favorite older person "perk" that people give you?
4. How do you imagine heaven?

[155] John 14:1-3

"But you be sober in all things, suffer hardship, do the work of an evangelist, and fulfill your ministry." - 2 Timothy 4:5

SPEAK, AND SOMETIMES USE WORDS

People often ask, "Why should we suffer. If we are saved why don't we just go straight to heaven?" The conventional answer is that we remain here to evangelize the world, and make disciples of all nations. The next question becomes, "How do we evangelize the world?" The answer is that there are many ways. Some Christians stand on street corners and shout, "Repent!" Others hand out Bible tracts. Many set up soup kitchens. A few paddle up remote jungle rivers. And lots of people go door to door.

In old age the question becomes, "What's the best way for me to evangelize that's a little less strenuous?" The answer will depend on the method of evangelization you've been taught. Most Christians have been raised thinking that evangelization is a sales process where people are persuaded to believe in Jesus by using logic and persuasive sales techniques. Which implies that nonbelievers are like consumers who must be shown why they are using the wrong product.

While methods of persuasion may work in a court of law, car dealership or the classroom where arguments of logical persuasion can sway a listener, we can't use logic or arm-twisting to awaken a person to divine truth. Persuasive techniques are only adequate to convince people to accept a different kind of laundry soap, philosophy, doctrine, dogma, religion or political ideology. But

Jesus is God; he cannot be sold in the marketplace of consumer comparison along with other commodities. He has no comparison. He is not a whimsical theory, vague philosophy or religious viewpoint that can be judged by our intellect. He is a truth that can only be accepted or rejected. He is a reality that can only be experienced based upon an experiential insight or event provided by the Holy Spirit. "I made known to them your name, and will make it known; that the love with which you loved me may be in them, and I in them."[156]

For example, when we point to the kitchen stove and say that it's hot, people can refute our statement and we can spend the rest of our day trying to convince them that it is. However, by simply placing their finger on the stove they will experience the heat for themselves. At which point there is no longer a debate, and no need for them to be convinced of the truth. In a similar way Jesus is a holy fire that must be personally touched, not argued about on a street corner, or in a sales presentation.

So how do we help people to touch the holy fire when we get older? Here's one way. We can offer every beat of our suffering heart for God's glory and he will take it and magnify our sacrifice in ways that we'll never understand. It's like taking the beating wings of a single butterfly in Brazil to create tiny ripples in the atmosphere that grow to become a tornado in Texas.[157] The butterfly never knows the magnitude that its tiny movement had upon people thousands of miles away.

---

[156] John 17:26

[157] From the "Butterfly Effect." A concept made popular by mathematician Edward Norton Lorenz, Sci-fi writer Ray Bradbury, and others.

But we've never heard the pastor say that God can use our suffering. We've been told that we are supposed to be doing mighty ministry activities as the working hands or evangelistic mouth of Christ. And we truly wanted to be used but now we've lost our teeth and our hands are swollen with arthritis.

We've never heard the minister say that maybe the best way to serve as part of the body of Christ would be as his aching back down at the clinic, his sore ankles hobbling into the grocery store, or his battered face at the skin specialist. We've never heard a sermon saying that our best witness might be found during a radiation treatment or while we are depressed as a rejected spirit.[158] And who wants to be Jesus' sorrowful soul?[159] Nobody I know.

We all want to evangelize the world seated comfortably by him as his personal advisor. We want people to see that we are his partner and confidant. We want our pal Jesus to promise us a safe, secure, and saved life. Of course we are dreaming, just as Saint Peter did to his embarrassment. "From that time, Jesus began to show his disciples that he must go to Jerusalem and suffer many things from the elders, chief priests, and scribes, and be killed, and the third day be raised up. Peter took him aside, and began to rebuke him, saying, "Far be it from you, Lord! This will never be done to you." But he turned, and said to Peter, "Get behind me, Satan! You are a stumbling block to me, for you are not setting your mind on the things of God, but on the things of men."[160]

---

[158] Isaiah 53:3
[159] Matthew 26:56
[160] Matthew 16:21-23

When we think that there is no need for us to join Jesus along the suffering road to the New Jerusalem, we set our mind upon the things of men. If we believe that a relationship with Jesus will bring us attention, comfort or happiness, we don't understand what he is doing. The overwhelming majority of all Christians will suffer in body, mind or soul at some point in their life. When we pick up our cross in old age and evangelize Jesus as his aching body, suffering spirit or lonely soul, God uses us as a living testimony to others. We will preach from a pulpit made of arthritis, heart disease, or osteoporosis. We will teach in a classroom formed of diabetes, bladder problems or cancer. And we will provide faith, hope and love to one another in a sanctuary created by anxiety, depression or some other horrible malady.

Granted, it will not be easy to give God the glory during a kidney dialysis. It will be difficult to smile on days we feel like screaming. It will be tough to walk with him when depression keeps us in bed. It will be hard to praise his name when we are hopelessly cynical. But if we decide to make the best of our sufferings, then we must ask what is our best? Our best will not be found in seeking sexual vitality, youthful looks, surfside mobility or athletic stamina. It will be found in being able to draw people's hand to the fire of Jesus by showing them that even though our body may be broken, Jesus holds us together in love; although our mind may be faltering, he proclaims his voice in hope; and even if our soul be wandering, he guides us in faith. That is how we will evangelize to the lost. They will come to know him by touching the fire of his suffering love by being touched by the fire of our suffering love.

Q's

1. What do you want, or expect from Jesus, as you grow older?
2. How do you define evangelization?
3. Do you ever evangelize? When and in what ways do you evangelize?
4. If you want to make the best of your suffering, then what is your best?

"For this is the message which you heard from the beginning, that we should love one another." ~ 1 John 3:11

BE GOD'S MESSENGER

In Steven Spielberg's movie Saving Private Ryan, there is a character called Captain Miller whose squad is pinned down by enemy fire. Miller needs a person to carry a message to some reinforcements located nearby. Miller's sergeant explains that the request is suicidal for any soldier, because the Germans snipers will single them out. But Captain Miller knows that the message is absolutely vital for their rescue. So he sends a volunteer messenger anyway.

Within seconds of leaving their safety behind a wall, the messenger is cut in half by a hail of machine gun fire. Everyone can see that he is dead. Suddenly, a second burst of automatic fire rakes his lifeless body. One of Miller's soldiers asks why the enemy would continue to fire on a dead man? Captain Miller explains that the Germans know that if the messenger has a single breath left in him, he can still carry the message.[161]

You are God's messenger. He has kept you alive for a particular purpose. The devil and his minions would like nothing more than to cut you down in old age with a hail of regrets, guilt, and other forms of spiritual doubt. Satan knows that you still carry a message from Jesus. He fears that you will tell others of the

---

[161] Saving Private Ryan, 1998. Amblin Entertainment. Steven Spielberg.

miracles you have seen, share the wisdom you have gained, teach essential lessons you have learned, or whisper your stories of experiencing God's liberating love.

Never doubt that you have a message about Jesus that no one else can deliver. And as long as your lungs have breath in them, you must deliver it. The ancient psalmist put it this way, "Yes, even when I am old and gray-haired, God, don't forsake me, until I have declared your strength to the next generation, and your might to everyone who is to come."[162]

Don't ask, "How can this be?" The power of God can make it be. Don't say, "I am not worthy to carry his message." No one is worthy to carry his message. Don't complain that, "I am too old" or "I am not useful." God doesn't see you through the lens of age, and he will find a use. Don't doubt that you have the words to say. God will give you the words you need. Don't fear. Profound theological arguments are for eager seminary students and their professors. Just "speak" the message of God's love through the smiling actions of your life whether you're in a wheelchair, hospital room, a dialysis center, or a visit with the grandchildren. Don't marvel. Your message is a simple response to an age-old question, "Sirs, what must I do to be saved?" Your answer will come through your suffering love that tells them, "Believe in the Lord Jesus Christ, and you will be saved, you and your household."[163]

---

[162] Psalm 71:18
[163] Acts 16:30-31

Q's

1. What message, or messages has God given to you?
2. Make a list of ways that you can deliver these messages.

"Beginning from the baptism of John, to the day that he was received up from us, of these one must become a witness with us of his resurrection." ~ Acts 1:22

BE GOD'S WITNESS

Accept your cross of suffering. Do it with the same desire, awareness, and trust that you had the day you first asked Jesus to be your savior. Recognize that you have a partner in pain with him. Understand that you can portion your sorrows, fears, and suffering with him. Know that you can live in the confidence that he has deliberately placed himself in the same leaky boat with you and will not allow the waters of darkness to overwhelm you. "When you pass through the waters, I will be with you; and through the rivers, they will not overflow you. When you walk through the fire, you will not be burned, and flame will not scorch you."[164]

Offer your sufferings to God by talking to him about them. Don't be afraid to get angry. He didn't punish Job for complaining, and he won't punish you. Besides, you can't tell him anything he doesn't already know, or anticipates. Be patient. He may answer you directly, or he may take his time. In the meantime, you may even be surprised to learn a few things about yourself and your situation that didn't occur to you.

Think about this. As you already know, Christians believe in

---

[164] Isaiah 43:2

intercessory prayer. That's when we offer our prayers to God on the behalf of others. But did you know that ancient Christians believed in intercessory suffering? That is when we offer our sufferings to God on behalf of others. Just as Jesus, offered his suffering to God as intercessory suffering on our behalf, we can offer our suffering to God as intercessory suffering on another's behalf, such as a hospitalized child, a suffering friend, or a wounded soldier.

Here are a few other things you might also want to consider in your old age.

- Just because we're older, it doesn't give us any special privileges, or right to be rude.

- Whenever you meet someone, treat them as if it's their last day on earth, not yours.

- Go out of your way to listen. You don't have to be a phony, but learn to have a genuine attitude of wanting to know something about the person you are speaking with. Then listen. Not for your enrichment, but for theirs. See how long you can go before saying a word.

- Practice the discipline of doing, not thinking. Don't just sit around and think all day about the past, or about what you'd like to do if only things were different.

- When the day is tough, make a list of five reasons why you are grateful to God. Save them for your children, and grand children to read so they might be blessed by your faith when you are gone.

- Contact someone you've been estranged from, such as a child, sibling or ex-spouse.

- Give people your encouragement and blessing. It costs you nothing, and it may change their life.

- Don't be discouraged. When your eyesight dims, look inside for light. When your hearing fails, listen to God's voice from within. Remember, you are not living to die, but dying to live. Your smallest sacrifice to further the love of God in this world will not go unrewarded.

- Work hard everyday to persevere in your suffering, because suffering is a way to participate in the ongoing life of Jesus. Believe that your suffering is a means to increase in God's grace. Trust that Jesus will use your suffering to reduce the suffering of others. Understand that suffering can bring you closer to God resulting in a complete reconciliation with him, or others no matter what your sins of the past.

God does not want us to give up in old age. It's not the time to lick our paws and feel sorry for ourselves. Instead, it's the time to rise up from our pallets, wheelchairs, and walkers to bring those around us our special message of hope, optimism, and truth as an older ambassador of God's suffering love.

Q's

1. How does Jesus partner in our pain?
2. Is it reasonable to believe that God would allow us to offer our suffering to mitigate the suffering of someone else? Is there any precedent in the Bible for it?
3. How would you contact someone you've been estranged from, such as a child, sibling or ex-spouse? Why would you do this?

THE ANCIENT WAY

By now, dear reader, you are probably depressed reading about the drab prospect of suffering, as we grow older. You may wonder where all the "good pleasing acceptable grand news" of the gospel is to be found within these pages. But that is precisely the point. When we move past trying to find the gospel of good feelings, we can discover the gospel of truth that explains our suffering predicament.

For all of us, the day of our departure is near. Until that day comes we may have to endure some suffering. If so, let's resolve to remain strong and steadfast no matter what happens. Saint Peter explains why, "For what glory is it if, when you sin, you patiently endure a beating? But if, when you do well, you patiently endure suffering, this is commendable with God."[165]

As a messenger of a God who suffers, let's minister to our friends, family, caregivers, and medical staff. Remind them that there is a God in heaven, and his name is Jesus. Let them witness what faithfulness looks like even during your difficult days. Show them your confidence in an eternal future. Pass along your spiritual wisdom, skills, and talents to those of the following generations so that the truth of Jesus never dims in America, or elsewhere.

We will not fear Satan but we will laugh at him on earth, just as we will laugh at him in heaven. We will dance in our hearts,

---

[165] 1 Peter 2:20

just as we will dance with the angels. We will sing gladness from our spirit, just as we will sing gladness with the saints above. And we will gladly share in Christ's suffering love now, as we will share in his suffering love forever.

And when our last breath finally comes, and Jesus leads us into his eternal kingdom, we will sing his praises along with billions of others who have gone before us, "You have turned my mourning into dancing for me. You have removed my sackcloth and clothed me with gladness, to the end that my heart may sing praise to you, and not be silent. Jesus my God, I will give thanks to you forever!"[166]

[166] Psalm 30:12

"My lips shall shout for joy! My soul, which you have redeemed, sings praises to you!" ~ *Psalm 71:23*

IS THAT ALL THERE IS?

I am much older than the rest of my family. Some time ago, I was driving with my daughter, and I explained that I would probably go to heaven while they were all still relatively young. She asked how I felt about that. I told her that except for my sadness at leaving them, it would be the best day of my life. I saw the shock on her face, until I explained that my death was the only certainty that I had ever known.

I went on to clarify that the day of my death would be the only day that I knew exactly what to expect. It would be the single most important event in my life. It would be the crowning moment that I had been created for. It would be the day when I would finally meet Jesus Christ face to face and at long last step into the splendor of his kingdom. How could I not look forward to meeting the person who had formed me in my mother's womb? What a joy to embrace and be embraced by the God I had often preached and taught about during my life?

There was a moment of silence in the car. Then she quietly replied, "But you're not leaving anytime soon, are you?"

"I don't think so," I said, laughing. "The Lord still has plenty of work for me to do. Like the Bible says, 'They will still bring forth fruit in old age. They will be full of sap and green, to show that Yahweh is upright.'"[167]

I realize that most of you readers don't feel the same way that I do about the end of your life. You may see your end and ask, "Is that all there is?" My answer is a resounding no. I have said it before, and I will repeat it; God is not preparing us to die, he is preparing us to live.

There will come a moment when the power of the Holy Spirit transforms us from the mortal beings we are into the immortal beings God intends. Saint Paul underscored the importance of this when he wrote, "That is why we are not discouraged. Though outwardly we are wearing out, inwardly we are renewed day by day. Our suffering is light and temporary and is producing for us an eternal glory that is greater than anything we can imagine."[168]

I realize that it will not be easy to finish our lives in a wheelchair, or a hospice bed. We will need help rolling away the stone from the darkened tomb of our mind. It may take enormous courage to slip away from the temple of our religion to find Jesus, who says, "You search the Scriptures, because you think that in them you have eternal life; and these are they which testify about me. Yet you refuse to come to me, that you may have life."[169]

When we finally do come to him, we will meet a suffering God who is no longer a pulpit fabrication woven from a cleric's imagination, or a caricature drawn from someone's best intentions. He will not be the wispy beta-male formed by the current cultural church. He will be as tough as solving Riemann's

---

[167] Psalm 92:14
[168] 2 Corinthians 4:6
[169] John 5:39

Hypothesis,[170] and softer than a mother's touch.

But most of all, he will be our long-suffering savior who has been living inside our hearts right under our nose patiently waiting for us to surrender our sacred illusions so that we can receive him as Truth. This will be the God of the ancient paths found at the end of our road when we are divested of our disguises, broken of our self-esteem, and utterly exposed before him.

And he will speak for himself, and we will listen to his voice as we shuffle about the house wearing our foam slippers. This will be the savior we have always wanted. This will be the God of our dreams. And after a lifetime of wandering, we will take our final steps with a God who says, "I will still be carrying you when you are old. Your hair will turn gray, and I will still carry you. I made you, and I will carry you to safety."[171]

---

[170] Considered the most difficult unsolved mathematical problem in the world.

[171] Isaiah 46:4

Made in the
USA
Middletown, DE